Structure and Architecture

Structure and Architecture

Angus J. Macdonald
Department of Architecture, University of Edinburgh

Second edition

Architectural Press

OXFORD   AUCKLAND   BOSTON   JOHANNESBURG   MELBOURNE   NEW DELHI

Architectural Press
An imprint of Butterworth-Heinemann
Linacre House, Jordan Hill, Oxford OX2 8DP
225 Wildwood Avenue, Woburn, MA 01801-2041
A division of Reed Educational and Professional Publishing Ltd

R   A member of the Reed Elsevier plc group

First published 1994
Reprinted 1995, 1996, 1997
Second edition 2001

British Library Cataloguing in Publication Data
Macdonald, Angus J.
    Structure and architecture. – 2nd ed.
    1. Structural design.   2. Architectural design
    I. Title
    721

ISBN 0 7506 4793 0

Library of Congress Cataloguing in Publication Data
A catalogue record for this book is available from the Library of Congress

€36.19

Printed and bound in Great Britain
Composition by Scribe Design, Gillingham, Kent

PLANT A TREE

British Trust for Conservation Volunteers

FOR EVERY VOLUME THAT WE PUBLISH, BUTTERWORTH-HEINEMANN
WILL PAY FOR BTCV TO PLANT AND CARE FOR A TREE.

Contents

Preface to the second edition

The major theme of this book is the relationship between structural design and architectural design. The various aspects of this are brought together in the last chapter which has been expanded in this second edition, partly in response to comments from readers of the first edition, partly because my own ideas have changed and developed, and partly as a consequence of discussion of the issues with colleagues in architecture and structural engineering. I have also added a section on the types of relationship which have existed between architects, builders and engineers, and on the influence which these have had on architectural style and form. The penultimate chapter, on structural criticism, has also been extensively rewritten. It is hoped that the ideas explored in both of these chapters will contribute to the better understanding of the essential and undervalued contribution of structural engineering to the Western architectural tradition and to present-day practice.

Angus J. Macdonald
Department of Architecture,
University of Edinburgh
December 2000

Acknowledgements

Angus Macdonald would like to thank all those, too numerous to mention, who have assisted in the making of this book. Special thanks are due to Stephen Gibson for his carefully crafted line drawings, Hilary Norman for her intelligent design, Thérèse Duriez for picture research and the staff of Architectural Press (and previously Butterworth-Heinemann) for their hard work and patience in initiating, editing and producing the book, particularly Neil Warnock-Smith, Diane Chandler, Angela Leopard, Siân Cryer and Sue Hamilton.

Illustrations other than those commissioned specially for the book are individually credited in their captions. Thanks are due to all those who supplied illustrations and especially to Pat Hunt, Tony Hunt, the late Alastair Hunter, Jill Hunter and the staff of the picture libraries of Ove Arup & Partners, Anthony Hunt Associates, the British Cement Association, the Architectural Association, the British Architecture Library and the Courtauld Institute.

Thanks are also due most particularly to my wife Pat, for her continued encouragement and for her expert scrutiny of the typescript.

Introduction

It has long been recognised that an appreciation of the role of structure is essential to the understanding of architecture. It was Vitruvius, writing at the time of the founding of the Roman Empire, who identified the three basic components of architecture as *firmitas*, *utilitas* and *venustas* and Sir Henry Wooton, in the seventeenth century[1], who translated these as 'firmness', 'commodity' and 'delight'. Subsequent theorists have proposed different systems by which buildings may be analysed, their qualities discussed and their meanings understood but the Vitruvian breakdown nevertheless still provides a valid basis for the examination and criticism of a building.

'Commodity', which is perhaps the most obvious of the Vitruvian qualities to appreciate, refers to the practical functioning of the building; the requirement that the set of spaces which is provided is actually useful and serves the purpose for which the building was intended. 'Delight' is the term for the effect of the building on the aesthetic sensibilities of those who come into contact with it. It may arise from one or more of a number of factors. The symbolic meanings of the chosen forms, the aesthetic qualities of the shapes, textures and colours, the elegance with which the various practical and programmatic problems posed by the building have been solved, and the ways in which links have been made between the different aspects of the design are all possible generators of 'delight'.

'Firmness' is the most basic quality. It is concerned with the ability of the building to preserve its physical integrity and survive in the world as a physical object. The part of the building which satisfies the need for 'firmness' is the structure. Structure is fundamental: without structure there is no building and therefore no 'commodity'. Without well-designed structure there can be no 'delight'.

To appreciate fully the qualities of a work of architecture the critic or observer should therefore know something of its structural make-up. This requires an intuitive ability to read a building as a structural object, a skill which depends on a knowledge of the functional requirements of structure and an ability to distinguish between the structural and the non-structural parts of the building. The first of these attributes can only be acquired by systematic study of those branches of mechanical science which are concerned with statics, equilibrium and the properties of materials. The second depends on a knowledge of buildings and how they are constructed. These topics are reviewed briefly in the preliminary chapters of this book.

The form of a structural armature is inevitably very closely related to that of the building which it supports, and the act of designing a building – of determining its overall form – is therefore also an act of structural design. The relationship between structural design and architectural design can take many forms however. At one extreme it is possible for an architect virtually to ignore structural considerations while inventing the form of a building and to conceal entirely the structural elements in the completed version of the building. The Statue of Liberty (Fig. ii) at the entrance to New York harbour, which, given that it contains an internal circulation system

---

1 Wooton, H., *The Elements of Architecture*, 1624.

of stairs and elevators, can be considered to be a building, is an example of this type. The buildings of early twentieth-century expressionism, such as the Einstein Tower at Potsdam by Mendelsohn (Fig. iii) and some recent buildings based on the ideas of Deconstruction (see Figs 1.11 and 7.41 to 7.44) might be cited as further examples.

All of these buildings contain a structure, but the technical requirements of the structure have not significantly influenced the form which has been adopted and the structural elements themselves are not important contributors to the aesthetics of the architecture. At the other extreme it is possible to produce a building which consists of little other than structure. The Olympic Stadium in Munich (Fig. i), by the architects Behnisch and Partners with Frei Otto, is an example of this. Between these extremes many different approaches to the relationship between structure and architecture are possible. In the 'high tech' architecture of the 1980s (Fig. iv), for example, the structural elements discipline the plan and general arrangement of the building and form an important part of the visual vocabulary. In the early Modern buildings of Gropius, Mies van der Rohe, Le Corbusier (see Fig. 7.34) and others, the forms which were adopted were greatly influenced by the types of geometry which were suitable for steel and reinforced concrete structural frameworks.

Fig. i Olympic Stadium, Munich, Germany, 1968–72; Behnisch & Partner, architects, with Frei Otto. In both the canopy and the raked seating most of what is seen is structural. (Photo: A. Macdonald)

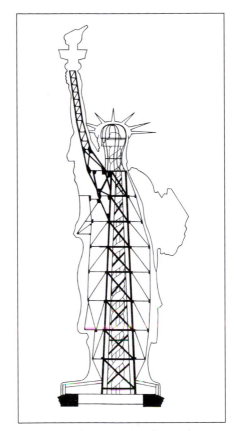

Fig. ii The thin external surface of the Statue of Liberty in New York Harbour, USA, is supported by a triangulated structural framework. The influence of structural considerations on the final version of the form was minimal.

Fig. iii Sketches by Mendelsohn of the Einstein Tower, Potsdam, Germany, 1917. Structural requirements had little influence on the external form of this building, although they did affect the internal planning. Surprisingly, it was constructed in loadbearing masonry.

The relationship between structure and architecture can therefore take many forms and it is the purpose of this book to explore these against a background of information concerning the technical properties and requirements of structures. The author hopes that it will be found useful by architectural critics and historians as well as students and practitioners of the professions concerned with building.

Fig. iv Inmos Microprocessor Factory, Newport, South Wales, 1982; Richard Rogers Partnership, architects; Anthony Hunt Associates, structural engineers. The general arrangement and appearance of this building were strongly influenced by the requirements of the exposed structure. The form of the latter was determined by space-planning requirements. (Photo: Anthony Hunt Associates)

Chapter 1

The relationship of structure to building

The simplest way of describing the function of an architectural structure is to say that it is the part of a building which resists the loads that are imposed on it. A building may be regarded as simply an envelope which encloses and subdivides space in order to create a protected environment. The surfaces which form the envelope, that is the walls, the floors and the roof of the building, are subjected to various types of loading. External surfaces are exposed to the climatic loads of snow, wind and rain; floors are subjected to the gravitational loads of the occupants and their effects; and most of the surfaces also have to carry their own weight (Fig. 1.1). All of these loads tend to distort the building envelope and to cause it to

collapse; it is to prevent this from happening that a structure is provided. The function of a structure may be summed up, therefore, as being to supply the strength and rigidity which are required to prevent a building from collapsing. More precisely, it is the part of a building which conducts the loads which are imposed on it from the points where they arise to the ground underneath the building, where they can ultimately be resisted.

The location of the structure within a building is not always obvious because the structure can be integrated with the non-structural parts in various ways. Sometimes, as in the simple example of an igloo (Fig. 1.2), in which ice blocks form a self-supporting protective dome, the structure and the space enclosing elements are one and the same thing. Sometimes the structural and space-enclosing elements are entirely separate. A very simple example is the tepee (Fig. 1.3), in which the protecting envelope is a skin of fabric or hide which has insufficient rigidity to form an enclosure by itself and which is supported on a framework of timber poles. Complete separation of structure and envelope occurs here: the envelope is entirely non-structural and the poles have a purely structural function.

The CNIT exhibition Hall in Paris (Fig. 1.4) is a sophisticated version of the igloo; the reinforced concrete shell which forms the main element of this enclosure is self-supporting and, therefore, structural. Separation of skin and structure occurs in the transparent walls, however, where the glass envelope is supported on a structure of mullions. The chapel by Le Corbusier at Ronchamp (see Fig. 7.40) is a similar example. The highly

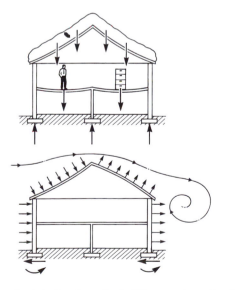

Fig. 1.1 Loads on the building envelope. Gravitational loads due to snow and to the occupation of the building cause roof and floor structures to bend and induce compressive internal forces in walls. Wind causes pressure and suction loads to act on all external surfaces.

Fig. 1.2   The igloo is a self-supporting compressive envelope.

Fig. 1.3   In the tepee a non-structural skin is supported on a structural framework of timber poles.

sculptured walls and roof of this building are made from a combination of masonry and reinforced concrete and are self-supporting. They are at the same time the elements which define the enclosure and the structural elements which give it the ability to maintain its form and resist load. The very large ice hockey arena at Yale by Saarinen (see Fig. 7.18) is yet another similar example. Here the building envelope consists of a network of steel cables which are suspended between three reinforced concrete arches, one in the vertical plane forming the spine of the building and two side arches almost in the horizontal plane. The composition of this building is more complex than in the previous cases because the suspended envelope can be broken down into the cable network, which has a purely structural function, and a non-structural cladding system. It might also be argued that the arches have a purely structural function and do not contribute directly to the enclosure of space.

The steel-frame warehouse by Foster Associates at Thamesmead, UK (Fig. 1.5), is almost a direct equivalent of the tepee. The elements which form it are either purely structural or entirely non-structural because

Fig. 1.4   Exhibition Hall of the CNIT, Paris, France; Nicolas Esquillan, architect. The principal element is a self-supporting reinforced concrete shell.

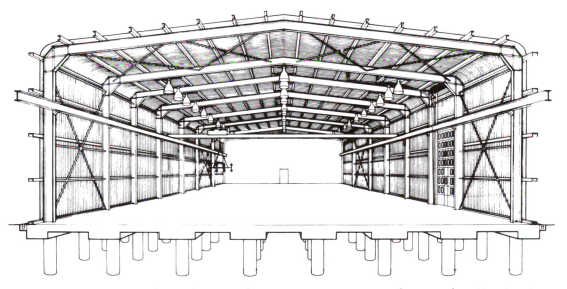

Fig. 1.5 Modern art glass warehouse, Thamesmead, UK, 1973; Foster Associates, architects; Anthony Hunt Associates, structural engineers. A non-structural skin of profiled metal sheeting is supported on a steel framework, which has a purely structural function. (Photo: Andrew Mead)

the corrugated sheet metal skin is entirely supported by the steel frame, which has a purely structural function. A similar breakdown may be seen in later buildings by the same architects, such as the Sainsbury Centre for the Visual Arts at Norwich and the warehouse and showroom for the Renault car company at Swindon (see Fig. 3.19).

In most buildings the relationship between the envelope and the structure is more complicated than in the above examples, and frequently this is because the interior of the building is subdivided to a greater extent by internal walls and floors. For instance, in Foster Associates' building for Willis, Faber and Dumas, Ipswich, UK (Figs 1.6 and 7.37),

3

the reinforced concrete structure of floor slabs and columns may be thought of as having a dual function. The columns are purely structural, although they do punctuate the interior spaces and are space-dividing elements, to some extent. The floors are both structural and space-dividing elements. Here, however, the situation is complicated by the fact that the structural floor slabs are topped by non-structural floor finishing materials and have ceilings suspended underneath them. The floor finishes and ceilings could be regarded as the true space-defining elements and the slab itself as having a purely structural function. The glass walls of the building are entirely non-structural and have a space-enclosing function only. The more recent Carré d'Art building in Nîmes (Fig. 1.7), also by Foster Associates, has a similar disposition of parts. As at Willis, Faber and Dumas a multi-storey reinforced concrete structure supports an external non-loadbearing skin.

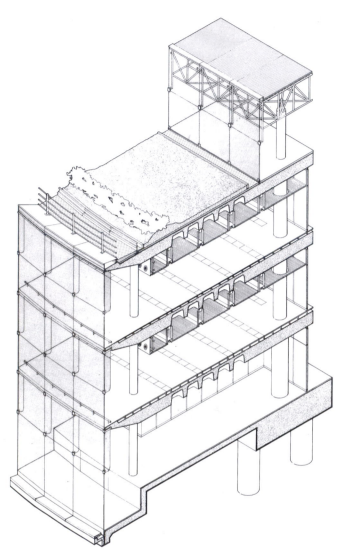

Fig. 1.6 Willis, Faber and Dumas Office, Ipswich, UK, 1974; Foster Associates, architects; Anthony Hunt Associates, structural engineers. The basic structure of this building is a series of reinforced concrete coffered slab floors supported on a grid of columns. The external walls are of glass and are non-structural. In the finished building the floor slabs are visible only at the perimeter. Elsewhere they are concealed by floor finishes and a false ceiling.

Fig. 1.7 Carré d'Art, Nîmes, France, 1993; Foster Associates, architects. A superb example of late twentieth-century Modernism. It has a reinforced concrete frame structure which supports a non-loadbearing external skin of glass. (Photo: James H. Morris)

The Antigone building at Montpellier by Ricardo Bofill (Fig. 1.8) is also supported by a multi-storey reinforced concrete framework. The facade here consists of a mixture of *in situ* and pre-cast concrete elements, and this, like the glass walls of the Willis, Faber and Dumas building, relies on a structural framework of columns and floor slabs for support. Although this building appears to be much more solid than those with fully glazed external walls it was constructed in a similar way. The Ulm Exhibition and Assembly Building by Richard Meier (Fig. 1.9) is also supported by a reinforced concrete structure. Here the structural continuity (see Appendix 3) and

Fig. 1.9 Ulm Exhibition and Assembly Building, Germany, 1986–93: Richard Meier & Partners, architects. The mouldability of concrete and the structural continuity which is a feature of this material are exploited here to produce a complex juxtaposition of solid and void. (Photo: E. & F. McLachlan)

Fig. 1.8 Antigone, Montpellier, France, 1983; Ricardo Bofill, architect. This building is supported by a reinforced concrete framework. The exterior walls are a combination of *in situ* and pre-cast concrete. They carry their own weight but rely on the interior framework for lateral support. (Photo: A. Macdonald)

mouldability which concrete offers were exploited to create a complex juxtaposition of solid and void. The building is of the same basic type as those by Foster and Bofill however; a structural framework of reinforced concrete supports cladding elements which are non-structural.

In the Centre Pompidou in Paris by Piano and Rogers, a multi-storey steel framework is used to support reinforced concrete floors and non-loadbearing glass walls. The breakdown of

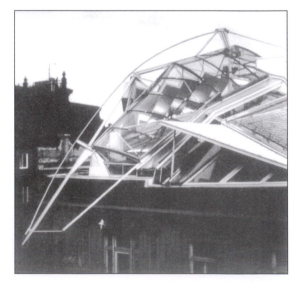

Fig. 1.10 Centre Pompidou, Paris, France, 1977; Piano & Rogers, architects; Ove Arup & Partners, structural engineers. The separation of structural and enclosing functions into distinct elements is obvious here. (Photo: A. Macdonald)

components positioned along the sides of the building outside the glass wall, which is attached to the frame near the columns. A system of cross-bracing on the sides of the framework prevents it from collapsing through instability.

The controlled disorder of the rooftop office extension in Vienna by Coop Himmelblau (Fig. 1.11) is in some respects a complete contrast to the controlled order of the Centre Pompidou. Architecturally it is quite different, expressing chaos rather than order, but structurally it is similar as the light external envelope is supported on a skeletal metal framework.

The house with masonry walls and timber floor and roof structures is a traditional form of building in most parts of the world. It is found in many forms, from the historic grand houses of the European landed aristocracy (Fig. 1.12) to modern homes in the UK (Figs 1.13 and 1.14). Even the simplest versions of this form of masonry and timber building (Fig. 1.13) are fairly complex assemblies of elements. Initial

parts is straightforward (Fig. 1.10): identical plane-frames, consisting of long steel columns which rise through the entire height of the building supporting triangulated girders at each floor level, are placed parallel to each other to form a rectangular plan. The concrete floors span between the triangulated girders. Additional small cast-steel girders project beyond the line of columns (Fig. 7.7) and are used to support stairs, escalators and servicing

Fig. 1.11 Rooftop office in Vienna, Austria, 1988; Coop Himmelblau, architects. The forms chosen here have no structural logic and were determined with almost no consideration for technical requirements. This approach design is quite feasible in the present day so long as the building is not too large.

Fig. 1.12 Château de Chambord, France, 1519–47. One of the grandest domestic buildings in Europe, the Château de Chambord has a loadbearing masonry structure. Most of the walls are structural; the floors are either of timber or vaulted masonry and the roof structure is of timber. (Photo: P. & A. Macdonald)

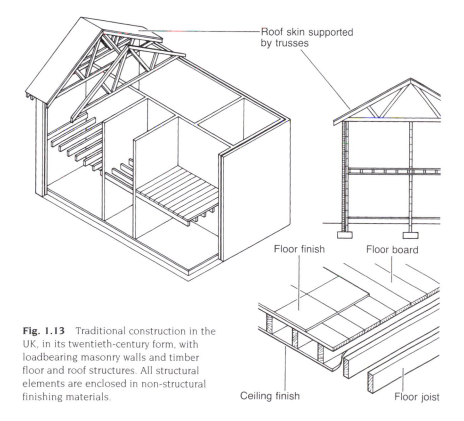

Roof skin supported by trusses

Floor finish

Floor board

Ceiling finish

Floor joist

Fig. 1.13 Traditional construction in the UK, in its twentieth-century form, with loadbearing masonry walls and timber floor and roof structures. All structural elements are enclosed in non-structural finishing materials.

7

consideration could result in a straightforward breakdown of parts with the masonry walls and timber floors being regarded as having both structural and space-dividing functions and the roof as consisting of a combination of the purely supportive trusses, which are the structural elements, and the purely protective, non-structural skin. Closer examination would reveal that most of the major elements can in fact be subdivided into parts which are either purely structural or entirely non-structural. The floors, for example, normally consist of an inner core of timber joists and floor boarding, which are the structural elements, enclosed by ceiling and floor finishes. The latter are the non-structural elements which are seen to divide the space. A similar breakdown is possible for the walls and in fact very little of what is visible in the traditional house is structural, as most of the structural elements are covered by non-structural finishes.

To sum up, these few examples of very different building types demonstrate that all buildings contain a structure, the function of which is to support the building envelope by conducting the forces which are applied to it from the points where they arise in the building to the ground below it where they are ultimately resisted. Sometimes the structure is indistinguishable from the enclosing and space-dividing building envelope, sometimes it is entirely separate from it; most often there is a mixture of elements with structural, non-structural and combined functions. In all cases the form of the structure is very closely related to that of the building taken as a whole and the elegance with which the structure fulfils its function is something which affects the quality of the architecture.

Fig. 1.14 Local authority housing, Haddington, Scotland, 1974; J. A. W. Grant, architects. These buildings have loadbearing masonry walls and timber floor and roof structures. (Photo: Alastair Hunter)

Chapter 2

Structural requirements

2.1 Introduction

To perform its function of supporting a building in response to whatever loads may be applied to it, a structure must possess four properties: it must be capable of achieving a state of equilibrium, it must be stable, it must have adequate strength and it must have adequate rigidity. The meanings of these terms are explained in this chapter. The influence of structural requirements on the forms which are adopted for structures is also discussed. The treatment is presented in a non-mathematical way and the definitions which are given are not those of the theoretical physicist; they are simply statements which are sufficiently precise to allow the significance of the concepts to structural design to be appreciated.

2.2 Equilibrium

Structures must be capable of achieving a state of equilibrium under the action of applied load. This requires that the internal configuration of the structure together with the means by which it is connected to its foundations must be such that all applied loads are balanced exactly by reactions generated at its foundations. The wheelbarrow provides a simple demonstration of the principles involved. When the wheelbarrow is at rest it is in a state of static equilibrium. The gravitational forces generated by its self weight and that of its contents act vertically downwards and are exactly balanced by reacting forces acting at the wheel and other supports. When a horizontal force is applied to the wheelbarrow by its operator it moves horizontally and is not therefore in a state of static equilibrium. This occurs because the interface between the wheelbarrow and the ground is incapable of generating horizontal reacting forces. The wheelbarrow is both a structure and a machine: it is a structure under the action of gravitational load and a machine under the action of horizontal load.

Despite the famous statement by one celebrated commentator, buildings are not machines[1]. Architectural structures must, therefore, be capable of achieving equilibrium under all directions of load.

2.3 Geometric stability

Geometric stability is the property which preserves the geometry of a structure and allows its elements to act together to resist load. The distinction between stability and equilibrium is illustrated by the framework shown in Fig. 2.1 which is capable of achieving a state of equilibrium under the action of gravitational load. The equilibrium is not stable, however, because the frame will collapse if disturbed laterally[2].

1   'A house is a machine for living.' Le Corbusier.
2   Stability can also be distinguished from strength or rigidity, because even if the elements of a structure have sufficient strength and rigidity to sustain the loads which are imposed on them, it is still possible for the system as a whole to fail due to its being geometrically unstable as is demonstrated in Fig. 2.1.

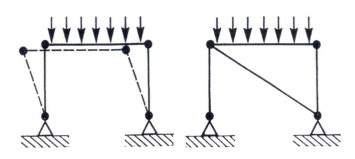

Fig. 2.1 A rectangular frame with four hinges is capable of achieving a state of equilibrium but is unstable because any slight lateral disturbance to the columns will induce it to collapse. The frame on the right here is stabilised by the diagonal element which makes no direct contribution to the resistance of the gravitational load.

This simple arrangement demonstrates that the critical factor, so far as the stability of any system is concerned, is the effect on it of a small disturbance. In the context of structures this is shown very simply in Fig. 2.2 by the comparison of tensile and compressive elements. If the alignment of either of these is disturbed, the tensile element is pulled back into line following the removal of the disturbing agency but the compressive element, once its initially perfect alignment has been altered, progresses to an entirely new position. The fundamental issue of stability is demonstrated here, which is that stable systems revert to their original state following a slight disturbance whereas unstable systems progress to an entirely new state.

The parts of structures which tend to be unstable are the ones in which compressive forces act and these parts must therefore be given special attention when the geometric stability of an arrangement is being considered. The columns in a simple rectangular framework are examples of this (Fig. 2.1). The three-dimensional bridge structure of Fig. 2.3 illustrates another potentially unstable system. Compression occurs in the horizontal elements in the upper parts of this frame when the weight of an object crossing the bridge is carried. The arrangement would fail by instability when this load was applied due to inadequate restraint of these compression parts. The compressive internal forces, which would inevitably occur

Original alignment

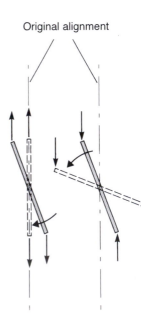

Fig. 2.2 The tensile element on the left here is stable because the loads pull it back into line following a disturbance. The compressive element on the right is fundamentally unstable.

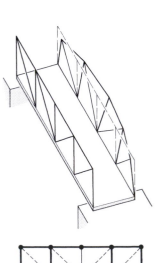

Fig. 2.3 The horizontal elements in the tops of the bridge girders are subjected to compressive internal force when the load is applied. The system is unstable and any eccentricity which is present initially causes an instability-type failure to develop.

——— Compression
------ Tension

with some degree of eccentricity, would push the upper elements out of alignment and cause the whole structure to collapse.

The geometric instability of the arrangements in Figures 2.1 and 2.3 would have been obvious if their response to horizontal load had been considered (Fig. 2.4). This demonstrates one of the fundamental requirements for the geometric stability of any arrangement of elements, which is that it must be capable of resisting loads from orthogonal directions (two orthogonal directions for plane arrangements and three for three-dimensional arrangements). This is another way of saying that an arrangement must be capable of achieving a state of equilibrium in response to forces from three orthogonal directions. The stability or otherwise of a proposed arrangement can therefore be judged by considering the effect on it of sets of mutually perpendicular trial forces: if the arrangement is capable of resisting all of these then it is stable, regardless of the loading pattern which will actually be applied to it in service.

Conversely, if an arrangement is not capable of resisting load from three orthogonal directions then it will be unstable in service even though the load which it is designed to resist will be applied from only one direction.

It frequently occurs in architectural design that a geometry which is potentially unstable must be adopted in order that other architectural requirements can be satisfied. For example, one of the most convenient structural geometries for buildings, that of the rectangular frame, is unstable in its simplest hinge-jointed form, as has already been shown. Stability can be achieved with this geometry by the use of rigid joints, by the insertion of a diagonal element or by the use of a rigid diaphragm which fills up the interior of the frame (Fig. 2.5). Each of these has disadvantages. Rigid joints are the most convenient from a space-planning point of view but are problematic structurally because they can render the structure statically indeterminate (see Appendix 3). Diagonal elements and diaphragms block the framework and can complicate space planning. In multi-panel arrangements, however, it is possible to produce stability without blocking every panel. The row of frames in Fig. 2.6, for example, is stabilised by the insertion of a single diagonal.

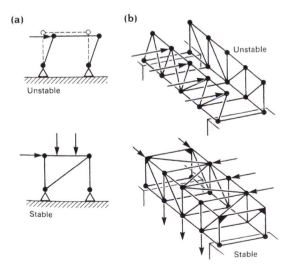

Fig. 2.4 Conditions for stability of frameworks. (a) The two-dimensional system is stable if it is capable of achieving equilibrium in response to forces from two mutually perpendicular directions. (b) The three-dimensional system is stable if it is capable of resisting forces from three directions. Note that in the case illustrated the resistance of transverse horizontal load is achieved by the insertion of rigid joints in the end bays.

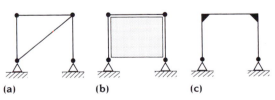

Fig. 2.5 A rectangular frame can be stabilised by the insertion of (a) a diagonal element or (b) a rigid diaphragm, or (c) by the provision of rigid joints. A single rigid joint is in fact sufficient to provide stability.

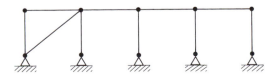

Fig. 2.6 A row of rectangular frames is stable if one panel only is braced by any of the three methods shown in Fig. 2.5.

Fig. 2.7 These frames contain the minimum number of braced panels required for stability.

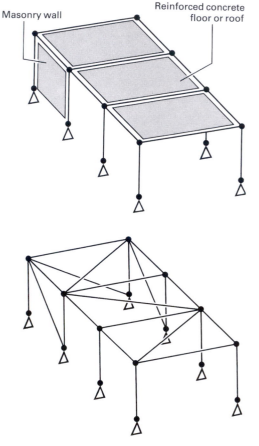

Masonry wall

Reinforced concrete floor or roof

Where frames are parallel to each other the three-dimensional arrangement is stable if a few panels in each of the two principal directions are stabilised in the vertical plane and the remaining frames are connected to these by diagonal elements or diaphragms in the horizontal plane (Fig. 2.7). A three-dimensional frame can therefore be stabilised by the use of diagonal elements or diaphragms in a limited number of panels in the vertical and horizontal planes. In multi-storey arrangements these systems must be provided at every storey level.

None of the components which are added to stabilise the geometry of the rectangular frame in Fig. 2.7 makes a direct contribution to the resistance of gravitational load (i.e. the carrying of weight, either of the structure itself or of the elements and objects which it supports). Such elements are called bracing elements. Arrangements which do not require bracing elements, either because they are fundamentally stable or because stability is provided by rigid joints, are said to be self-bracing.

Most structures contain bracing elements whose presence frequently affects both the initial planning and the final appearance of the building which it supports. The issue of stability, and in particular the design of bracing systems, is therefore something which affects the architecture of buildings.

Where a structure is subjected to loads from different directions, the elements which are used solely for bracing when the principal load is applied frequently play a direct role in resisting secondary load. The diagonal elements in the frame of Fig. 2.7, for example, would be directly involved in the resistance of any horizontal load which was applied, such as might occur due to the action of wind. Because real structures are usually subjected to loads from different directions, it is very rare for elements to be used solely for bracing.

The nature of the internal force in bracing components depends on the direction in which the instability which they prevent occurs. In Fig. 2.8, for example, the diagonal element will be placed in tension if the frame sways to the right and in compression if it sways to the left. Because the direction of sway due to instability cannot be predicted when the structure is being designed, the single bracing element would have to be made strong enough to carry either tension or compression. The resistance of compression requires a much larger size of cross-section than that of tension, however, especially if the element is long[3], and this is a critical factor in determining its size. It is normally more economical to insert both diagonal elements into a rectangular frame

3 This is because compression elements can suffer from the buckling phenomenon. The basic principles of this are explained in elementary texts on structures such as Engel, H., *Structural Principles*, Prentice-Hall, Englewood Cliffs, NJ, 1984. See also Macdonald, Angus J., *Structural Design for Architecture*, Architectural Press, Oxford, 1997, Appendix 2.

(cross-bracing) than a single element and to design both of them as tension-only elements. When the panel sways due to instability the element which is placed in compression simply buckles slightly and the whole of the restraint is provided by the tension diagonal.

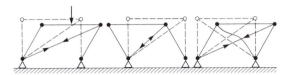

Fig. 2.8 Cross-bracing is used so that sway caused by instability is always resisted by a diagonal element acting in tension. The compressive diagonal buckles slightly and carries no load.

It is common practice to provide more bracing elements than the minimum number required so as to improve the resistance of three-dimensional frameworks to horizontal load. The framework in Fig. 2.7, for example, although theoretically stable, would suffer considerable distortion in response to a horizontal load applied parallel to the long side of the frame at the opposite end from the vertical-plane bracing. A load applied parallel to the long side at this end of the frame would also cause a certain amount of distress as some movement of joints would inevitably occur in the transmission of it to the vertical-plane bracing at the other end. In practice the performance of the frame is more satisfactory if vertical-plane bracing is provided at both ends (Fig. 2.9). This gives more restraint than is necessary for stability and makes the structure statically indeterminate (see Appendix 3), but results in the horizontal loads being resisted close to the points where they are applied to the structure.

Another practical consideration in relation to the bracing of three-dimensional rectangular frames is the length of the diagonal elements which are provided. These sag in response to their own weight and it is therefore advantageous to make them as short as possible. For this reason bracing elements are frequently restricted to a part of the panel in which they are located. The frame shown in Fig. 2.10 contains this refinement.

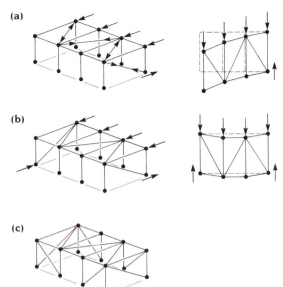

Fig. 2.9 In practical bracing schemes more elements than are strictly necessary to ensure stability are provided to improve the performance of frameworks in resisting horizontal load. Frame (a) is stable but will suffer distortion in response to horizontal load on the side walls. Its performance is enhanced if a diagonal element is provided in both end walls (b). The lowest framework (c) contains the minimum number of elements required to resist effectively horizontal load from the two principal horizontal directions. Note that the vertical-plane bracing elements are distributed around the structure in a symmetrical configuration.

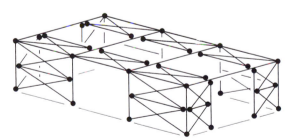

Fig. 2.10 In practice, bracing elements are frequently confined to a part of each panel only.

Figures 2.11 and 2.12 show typical bracing systems for multi-storey frameworks. Another common arrangement, in which floor slabs act as diaphragm-type bracing in the horizontal plane in conjunction with vertical-plane bracing of the diagonal type, is shown in Fig. 2.13. When the rigid-joint method is used it is

13

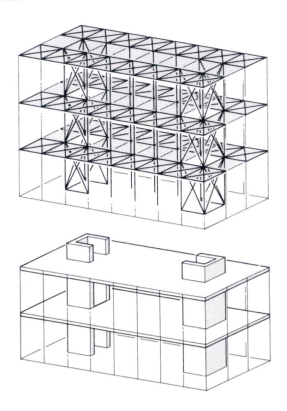

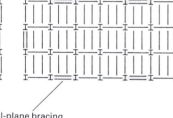

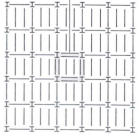

Fig. 2.11 A typical bracing scheme for a multi-storey framework. Vertical-plane bracing is provided in a limited number of bays and positioned symmetrically on plan. All other bays are linked to this by diagonal bracing in the horizontal plane at every storey level.

normal practice to stabilise all panels individually by making all joints rigid. This eliminates the need for horizontal-plane bracing altogether, although the floors normally act to distribute through the structure any unevenness in the application of horizontal load. The rigid-joint method is the normal method which is adopted for reinforced concrete frames, in which continuity through junctions between elements can easily be achieved; diaphragm bracing is also used, however, in both vertical and horizontal planes in certain types of reinforced concrete frame.

Loadbearing wall structures are those in which the external walls and internal partitions serve as vertical structural elements. They are normally constructed of masonry, reinforced

Fig. 2.12 These drawings of floor grid patterns for steel frameworks show typical locations for vertical-plane bracing.

Vertical-plane bracing

Vertical-plane bracing

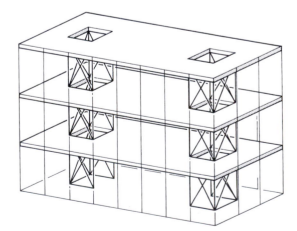

Fig. 2.13 Concrete floor slabs are normally used as horizontal-plane bracing of the diaphragm type which acts in conjunction with diagonal bracing in the vertical planes.

concrete or timber, but combinations of these materials are also used. In all cases the joints between walls and floors are normally incapable of resisting bending action (in other words they behave as hinges) and the resulting lack of continuity means that rigid-frame action cannot develop. Diaphragm bracing, provided by the walls themselves, is used to stabilise these structures.

A wall panel has high rotational stability in its own plane but is unstable in the out-of-plane direction (Fig. 2.14); vertical panels must, therefore, be grouped in pairs at right

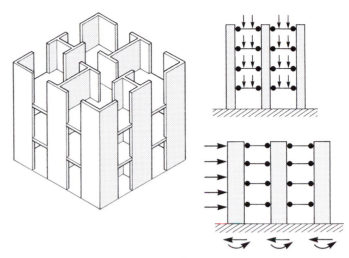

Fig. 2.15 Loadbearing masonry buildings are normally multi-cellular structures which contain walls running in two orthogonal directions. The arrangement is inherently stable.

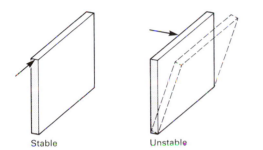

Stable   Unstable

Stable

Fig. 2.14 Walls are unstable in the out-of-plane direction and must be grouped into orthogonal arrangements for stability.

angles to each other so that they provide mutual support. For this to be effective the structural connection which is provided in the vertical joint between panels must be capable of resisting shear[4]. Because loadbearing wall structures are normally used for multi-cellular buildings, the provision of an adequate number of vertical-plane bracing diaphragms

in two orthogonal directions is normally straightforward (Fig. 2.15). It is unusual therefore for bracing requirements to have a significant effect on the internal planning of this type of building.

The need to ensure that a structural framework is adequately braced is a factor that can affect the internal planning of buildings. The basic requirement is that some form of bracing must be provided in three orthogonal planes. If diagonal or diaphragm bracing is used in the vertical planes this must be accommodated within the plan. Because vertical-plane bracing is most effective when it is arranged symmetrically, either in internal cores or around the perimeter of the building, this can affect the space planning especially in tall buildings where the effects of wind loading are significant.

2.4 Strength and rigidity

2.4.1 Introduction

The application of load to a structure generates internal forces in the elements and external reacting forces at the foundations (Fig. 2.16) and the elements and foundations must

---

4 See Engel, H., *Structural Principles*, Prentice-Hall, Englewood Cliffs, NJ, 1984 for an explanation of shear.

15

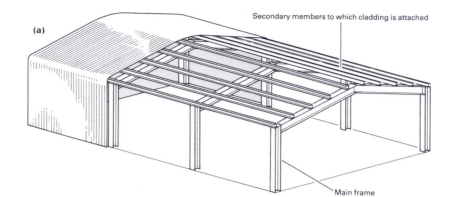

Secondary members to which cladding is attached

Main frame

Fig. 2.16 The structural elements of a building conduct the loads to the foundations. They are subjected to internal forces that generate stresses the magnitudes of which depend on the intensities of the internal forces and the sizes of the elements. The structure will collapse if the stress levels exceed the strength of the material.

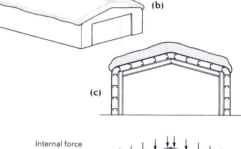

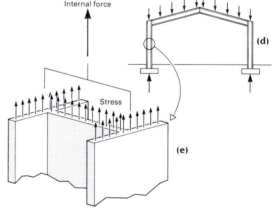

have sufficient strength and rigidity to resist these. They must not rupture when the peak load is applied; neither must the deflection which results from the peak load be excessive.

The requirement for adequate strength is satisfied by ensuring that the levels of stress which occur in the various elements of a structure, when the peak loads are applied, are within acceptable limits. This is chiefly a matter of providing elements with cross-sections of adequate size, given the strength of the constituent material. The determination of the sizes required is carried out by structural calculations. The provision of adequate rigidity is similarly dealt with.

Structural calculations allow the strength and rigidity of structures to be controlled precisely. They are preceded by an assessment of the load which a structure will be required to carry. The calculations can be considered to be divisible into two parts and to consist firstly of the structural analysis, which is the evaluation of the internal forces which occur in the elements of the structure, and secondly, the element-sizing calculations which are carried out to ensure that they will have sufficient strength and rigidity to resist the internal forces which the loads will cause. In many cases, and always for statically

indeterminate structures (see Appendix 3), the two sets of calculations are carried out together, but it is possible to think of them as separate operations and they are described separately here.

2.4.2 The assessment of load

The assessment of the loads which will act on a structure involves the prediction of all the different circumstances which will cause load to be applied to a building in its lifetime (Fig. 2.17) and the estimation of the greatest

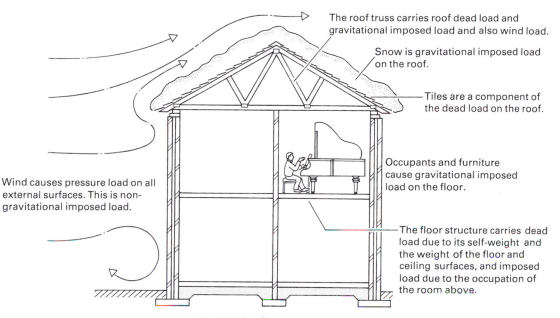

The roof truss carries roof dead load and gravitational imposed load and also wind load.

Snow is gravitational imposed load on the roof.

Tiles are a component of the dead load on the roof.

Occupants and furniture cause gravitational imposed load on the floor.

Wind causes pressure load on all external surfaces. This is non-gravitational imposed load.

The floor structure carries dead load due to its self-weight and the weight of the floor and ceiling surfaces, and imposed load due to the occupation of the room above.

Fig. 2.17 The prediction of the maximum load which will occur is one of the most problematic aspects of structural calculations. Loading standards are provided to assist with this but assessment of load is nevertheless one of the most imprecise parts of the structural calculation process.

magnitudes of these loads. The maximum load could occur when the building was full of people, when particularly heavy items of equipment were installed, when it was exposed to the force of exceptionally high winds or as a result of many other eventualities. The designer must anticipate all of these possibilities and also investigate all likely combinations of them.

The evaluation of load is a complex process, but guidance is normally available to the designer of a structure from loading standards[5]. These are documents in which data and wisdom gained from experience are presented systematically in a form which allows the information to be applied in design.

2.4.3 The analysis calculations

The purpose of structural analysis is to determine the magnitudes of all of the forces, internal and external, which occur on and in a

structure when the most unfavourable load conditions occur. To understand the various processes of structural analysis it is necessary to have a knowledge of the constituents of structural force systems and an appreciation of concepts, such as equilibrium, which are used to derive relationships between them. These topics are discussed in Appendix 1.

In the analysis of a structure the external reactions which act at the foundations and the internal forces in the elements are calculated from the loads. This is a process in which the structure is reduced to its most basic abstract form and considered separately from the rest of the building which it will support.

An indication of the sequence of operations which are carried out in the analysis of a simple structure is given in Fig. 2.18. After a preliminary analysis has been carried out to evaluate the external reactions, the structure is subdivided into its main elements by making 'imaginary cuts' (see Appendix 1.7) through the junctions between them. This creates a set of 'free-body-diagrams' (Appendix 1.6) in which the forces that act between the elements are

---

5 In the UK the relevant standard is BS 6399, *Design Loading for Buildings*, British Standards Institution, 1984.

17

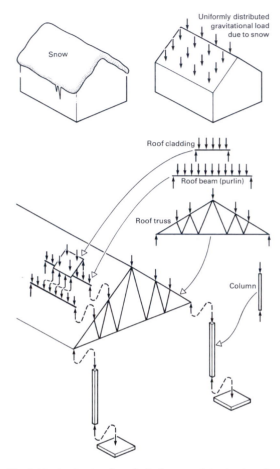

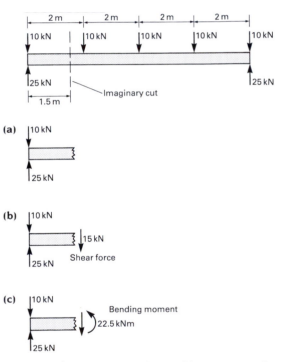

Fig. 2.18 In structural analysis the complete structure is broken down into two-dimensional components and the internal forces in these are subsequently calculated. The diagram shows the pattern forces which result from gravitational load on the roof of a small building. Similar breakdowns are carried out for the other forms of load and a complete picture is built up of the internal forces which will occur in each element during the life of the structure.

exposed. Following the evaluation of these inter-element forces the individual elements are analysed separately for their internal forces by further applications of the 'imaginary cut' technique. In this way all of the internal forces in the structure are determined.

In large, complex, statically indeterminate structures the magnitudes of the internal forces are affected by the sizes and shapes of the element cross-sections and the properties of the constituent materials, as well as by the magnitudes of the loads and the overall

geometry of the structure. The reason for this is explained in Appendix 3. In these circumstances the analysis and element-sizing calculations are carried out together in a trial and error process which is only feasible in the context of computer-aided design.

The different types of internal force which can occur in a structural element are shown in Fig. 2.19. As these have a very significant influence on the sizes and shapes which are specified for elements they will be described briefly here.

In Fig. 2.19 an element is cut through at a particular cross-section. In Fig. 2.19(a) the forces which are external to one of the

Fig. 2.19 The investigation of internal forces in a simple beam using the device of the 'imaginary cut'. The cut produces a free-body-diagram from which the nature of the internal forces at a single cross-section can be deduced. The internal forces at other cross-sections can be determined from similar diagrams produced by cuts made in appropriate places. (a) Not in equilibrium. (b) Positional equilibrium but not in rotational equilibrium. (c) Positional and rotational equilibrium. The shear force on the cross-section 1.5 m from the left-hand support is 15 kN; the bending moment on this cross-section is 22.5 kNm.

resulting sub-elements are marked. If these were indeed the only forces which acted on the sub-element it would not be in a state of equilibrium. For equilibrium the forces must balance and this is clearly not the case here; an additional vertical force is required for equilibrium. As no other external forces are present on this part of the element the extra force must act on the cross-section where the cut occurred. Although this force is external to the sub-element it is an internal force so far as the complete element is concerned and is called the 'shear force'. Its magnitude at the cross-section where the cut was made is simply the difference between the external forces which occur to one side of the cross-section, i.e. to the left of the cut.

Once the shear force is added to the diagram the question of the equilibrium of the sub-element can once more be examined. In fact it is still not in a state of equilibrium because the set of forces now acting will produce a turning effect on the sub-element which will cause it to rotate in a clockwise sense. For equilibrium an anti-clockwise moment is required and as before this must act on the cross-section at the cut because no other external forces are present. The moment which acts at the cut and which is required to establish rotational equilibrium is called the bending moment at the cross-section of the cut. Its magnitude is obtained from the moment equation of equilibrium for the free-body-diagram. Once this is added to the diagram the system is in a state of static equilibrium, because all the conditions for equilibrium are now satisfied (see Appendix 1).

Shear force and bending moment are forces which occur inside structural elements and they can be defined as follows. The shear force at any location is the amount by which the external forces acting on the element, to one side of that location, do not balance when they are resolved perpendicular to the axis of the element. The bending moment at a location in an element is the amount by which the moments of the external forces acting to one side of the location, about any point in their

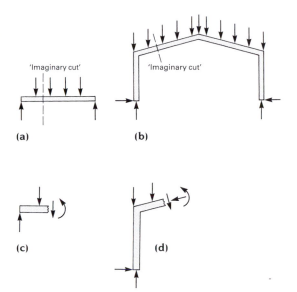

Fig. 2.20 The 'imaginary cut' is a device for exposing internal forces and rendering them susceptible to equilibrium analysis. In the simple beam shown here shear force and bending moment are the only internal forces required to produce equilibrium in the element isolated by the cut. These are therefore the only internal forces which act on the cross-section at which the cut was made. In the case of the portal frame, axial thrust is also required at the cross-section exposed by the cut.

plane, do not balance. Shear force and bending moment occur in structural elements which are bent by the action of the applied load. Beams and slabs are examples of such elements.

One other type of internal force can act on the cross-section of an element, namely axial thrust (Fig. 2.20). This is defined as the amount by which the external forces acting on the element to one side of a particular location do not balance when they are resolved parallel to the direction of the element. Axial thrust can be either tensile or compressive.

In the general case each cross-section of a structural element is acted upon by all three internal forces, namely shear force, bending moment and axial thrust. In the element-sizing part of the calculations, cross-section sizes are determined that ensure the levels of stress which these produce are not excessive. The efficiency with which these internal forces can be resisted depends on the shape of the cross-section (see Section 4.2).

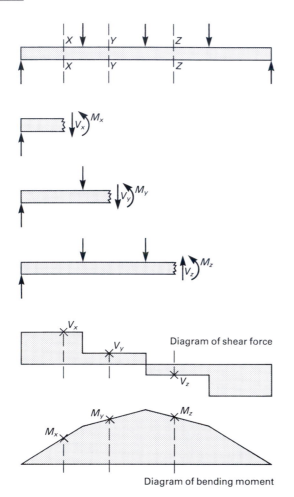

Fig. 2.21 The magnitudes of internal forces normally vary along the length of a structural element. Repeated use of the 'imaginary cut' technique yields the pattern of internal forces in this simple beam.

The magnitudes of the internal forces in structural elements are rarely constant along their lengths, but the internal forces at any cross-section can always be found by making an 'imaginary cut' at that point and solving the free-body-diagram which this creates. Repeated applications of the 'imaginary cut' technique at different cross-sections (Fig. 2.21) allows the full pattern of internal forces to be evaluated. In present-day practice these calculations are processed by computer and the results presented graphically in the form of bending moment, shear force and axial thrust diagrams for each structural element.

The shapes of bending moment, shear force and axial thrust diagrams are of great significance for the eventual shapes of structural elements because they indicate the locations of the parts where greatest strength will be required. Bending moment is normally large in the vicinity of mid-span and near rigid joints. Shear force is highest near support joints. Axial thrust is usually constant along the length of structural elements.

2.4.4 Element-sizing calculations

The size of cross-section which is provided for a structural element must be such as to give it adequate strength and adequate rigidity. In other words, the size of the cross-section must allow the internal forces determined in the analysis to be carried without overloading the structural material and without the occurrence of excessive deflection. The calculations which are carried out to achieve this involve the use of the concepts of stress and strain (see Appendix 2).

In the sizing calculations each element is considered individually and the area of cross-section determined which will maintain the stress at an acceptable level in response to the peak internal forces. The detailed aspects of the calculations depend on the type of internal force and, therefore, the stress involved and on the properties of the structural material.

As with most types of design the evolution of the final form and dimensions of a structure is, to some extent, a cyclic process. If the element-sizing procedures yield cross-sections which are considered to be excessively large or unsuitable in some other way, modification of the overall form of the structure will be undertaken so as to redistribute the internal forces. Then, the whole cycle of analysis and element-sizing calculations must be repeated.

If a structure has a geometry which is stable and the cross-sections of the elements are sufficiently large to ensure that it has adequate strength it will not collapse under the action of the loads which are applied to it. It will therefore be safe, but this does not necessarily mean that its performance will be satisfactory (Fig. 2.22). It may suffer a large amount of

Fig. 2.22 A structure with adequate strength will not collapse, but excessive flexibility can render it unfit for its purpose.

deflection under the action of the load and any deformation which is large enough to cause damage to brittle building components, such as glass windows, or to cause alarm to the building's occupants or even simply to cause unsightly distortion of the building's form is a type of structural failure.

The deflection which occurs in response to a given application of load to a structure depends on the sizes of the cross-sections of the elements[6] and can be calculated once element dimensions have been determined. If the sizes which have been specified to provide adequate strength will result in excessive deflection they are increased by a suitable amount. Where this occurs it is the rigidity requirement which is critical and which determines the sizes of the structural elements. Rigidity is therefore a phenomenon which is not directly related to strength; it is a

separate issue and is considered separately in the design of structures.

2.5 Conclusion

In this chapter the factors which affect the basic requirements of structures have been reviewed. The achievement of stable equilibrium has been shown to be dependent largely on the geometric configuration of the structure and is therefore a consideration which affects the determination of its form. A stable form can almost always be made adequately strong and rigid, but the form chosen does affect the efficiency with which this can be accomplished. So far as the provision of adequate strength is concerned the task of the structural designer is straightforward, at least in principle. He or she must determine by analysis of the structure the types and magnitudes of the internal forces which will occur in all of the elements when the maximum load is applied. Cross-section shapes and sizes must then be selected such that the stress levels are maintained within acceptable limits. Once the cross-sections have been determined in this way the structure will be adequately strong. The amount of deflection which will occur under the maximum load can then be calculated. If this is excessive the element sizes are increased to bring the deflection within acceptable limits. The detailed procedures which are adopted for element sizing depend on the types of internal force which occur in each part of the structure and on the properties of the structural materials.

---

6   The deflection of a structure is also dependent on the properties of the structural material and on the overall configuration of the structure.

Chapter 3

Structural materials

3.1 Introduction

The shapes which are adopted for structural elements are affected, to a large extent, by the nature of the materials from which they are made. The physical properties of materials determine the types of internal force which they can carry and, therefore, the types of element for which they are suitable. Unreinforced masonry, for example, may only be used in situations where compressive stress is present. Reinforced concrete performs well when loaded in compression or bending, but not particularly well in axial tension.

The processes by which materials are manufactured and then fashioned into structural elements also play a role in determining the shapes of elements for which they are suitable. These aspects of the influence of material properties on structural geometry are now discussed in relation to the four principal structural materials of masonry, timber, steel and reinforced concrete.

3.2 Masonry

Masonry is a composite material in which individual stones, bricks or blocks are bedded in mortar to form columns, walls, arches or vaults (Fig. 3.1). The range of different types of masonry is large due to the variety of types of constituent. Bricks may be of fired clay, baked earth, concrete, or a range of similar materials, and blocks, which are simply very large bricks, can be similarly composed. Stone too is not one but a very wide range of materials, from the relatively soft sedimentary rocks such as limestone to the very hard granites and other

igneous rocks. These 'solid' units can be used in conjunction with a variety of different mortars to produce a range of masonry types. All have certain properties in common and therefore produce similar types of structural element. Other materials such as dried mud, pisé or even unreinforced concrete have similar properties and can be used to make similar types of element.

The physical properties which these materials have in common are moderate compressive strength, minimal tensile strength and relatively high density. The very low tensile strength restricts the use of masonry to elements in which the principal internal force is compressive, i.e. columns, walls and compressive form-active types (see Section 4.2) such as arches, vaults and domes.

In post-and-beam forms of structure (see Section 5.2) it is normal for only the vertical elements to be of masonry. Notable exceptions are the Greek temples (see Fig. 7.1), but in these the spans of such horizontal elements as are made in stone are kept short by subdivision of the interior space by rows of columns or walls. Even so, most of the elements which span horizontally are in fact of timber and only the most obvious, those in the exterior walls, are of stone. Where large horizontal spans are constructed in masonry compressive form-active shapes must be adopted (Fig. 3.1).

Where significant bending moment occurs in masonry elements, for example as a consequence of side thrusts on walls from rafters or vaulted roof structures or from out-of-plane wind pressure on external walls, the level of tensile bending stress is kept low by making the second moment of area (see Appendix 2) of

Fig. 3.1 Chartres Cathedral, France, twelfth and thirteenth centuries. The Gothic church incorporates most of the various forms for which masonry is suitable. Columns, walls and compressive form-active arches and vaults are all visible here. (Photo: Courtauld Institute)

the cross-section large. This can give rise to very thick walls and columns and, therefore, to excessively large volumes of masonry unless some form of 'improved' cross-section (see Section 4.3) is used. Traditional versions of this are buttressed walls. Those of medieval Gothic cathedrals or the voided and sculptured walls which support the large vaulted enclosures of Roman antiquity (see Figs 7.30 to 7.32) are among the most spectacular examples. In all of these the volume of masonry is small in relation to the total effective thickness of the wall concerned. The fin and diaphragm walls of recent tall single-storey masonry buildings (Fig. 3.2) are twentieth-century equivalents. In the modern buildings the bending moments which occur in the walls are caused principally by wind loading and not by the lateral thrusts from roof structures. Even where 'improved' cross-sections are adopted the volume of material in a masonry structure is usually large and produces walls and vaults which act as

23

(a)

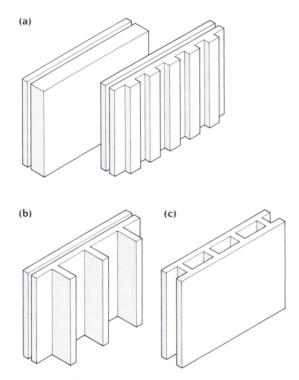

(b)   **(c)**

Fig. 3.2 Where masonry will be subjected to significant bending moment, as in the case of external walls exposed to wind loading, the overall thickness must be large enough to ensure that the tensile bending stress is not greater than the compressive stress caused by the gravitational load. The wall need not be solid, however, and a selection of techniques for achieving thickness efficiently is shown here.

effective thermal, acoustic and weathertight barriers.

The fact that masonry structures are composed of very small basic units makes their construction relatively straightforward. Subject to the structural constraints outlined above, complex geometries can be produced relatively easily, without the need for sophisticated plant or techniques and very large structures can be built by these simple means (Fig. 3.3). The only significant constructional drawback of masonry is that horizontal-span structures such as arches and vaults require temporary support until complete.

Other attributes of masonry-type materials are that they are durable, and can be left exposed in both the interiors and exteriors of buildings. They are also, in most locations, available locally in some form and do not therefore require to be transported over long distances. In other words, masonry is an environmentally friendly material the use of which must be expected to increase in the future.

Fig. 3.3 Town Walls, Igerman, Iran. This late mediaeval brickwork structure demonstrates one of the advantages of masonry, which is that very large constructions with complex geometries can be achieved by relatively simple building processes.

3.3 Timber

Timber has been used as a structural material from earliest times. It possesses both tensile and compressive strength and, in the structural role is therefore suitable for elements which carry axial compression, axial tension and bending-type loads. Its most widespread application in architecture has been in buildings of domestic scale in which it has been used to make complete structural frameworks, and for the floors and roofs in loadbearing masonry structures. Rafters, floor beams, skeleton frames, trusses, built-up beams of various kinds, arches, shells and folded forms have all been constructed in timber (Figs 3.4, 3.6, 3.9 and 3.10).

The fact of timber having been a living organism is responsible for the nature of its physical properties. The parts of the tree which are used for structural timber – the heartwood and sapwood of the trunk – have a structural function in the living tree and therefore have, in common with most organisms, very good structural properties. The material is composed of long fibrous cells aligned parallel to the original tree trunk and therefore to the grain which results from the annual rings. The material of the cell walls gives timber its strength and the fact that its constituent elements are of low atomic weight is responsible for its low density. The lightness in weight of timber is also due to its cellular internal structure which produces element cross-sections which are permanently 'improved' (see Section 4.3).

Parallel to the grain, the strength is approximately equal in tension and compression so that planks aligned with the grain can be used for elements which carry axial compression, axial tension or bending-type loads as noted above. Perpendicular to the grain it is much less strong because the fibres are easily crushed or pulled apart when subjected to compression or tension in this direction.

This weakness perpendicular to the grain causes timber to have low shear strength when subjected to bending-type loads and also makes it intolerant of the stress concentrations

Fig. 3.4 Methodist church, Haverhill, Suffolk, UK; J. W. Alderton, architect. A series of laminated timber portal frames is used here to provide a vault-like interior. Timber is also used for secondary structural elements and interior lining. (Photo: S. Baynton)

such as occur in the vicinity of mechanical fasteners such as bolts and screws. This can be mitigated by the use of timber connectors, which are devices designed to increase the area of contact through which load is transmitted in a joint. Many different designs of timber connector are currently available (Fig. 3.5) but, despite their development, the difficulty of making satisfactory structural connections with mechanical fasteners is a factor which limits the load carrying capacity of timber elements, especially tensile elements.

The development in the twentieth century of structural glues for timber has to some extent solved the problem of stress concentration at joints, but timber which is to be glued must be very carefully prepared if the joint is to develop its full potential strength and the curing of the glue must be carried out under controlled conditions of temperature and relative humidity[1]. This is impractical on building sites

---

1   A good explanation of the factors which affect the gluing of timber can be found in Gordon, J. E., *The New Science of Strong Materials*, Penguin, London, 1968.

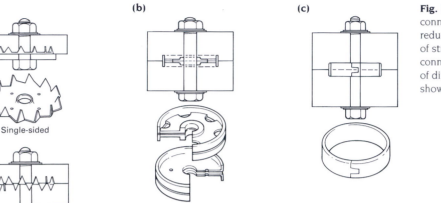

(a)

Single-sided

Double-sided

(b)

(c)

Fig. 3.5 Timber connectors are used to reduce the concentration of stress in bolted connections. A selection of different types is shown here.

and has to be regarded as a pre-fabricating technique.

Timber suffers from a phenomenon known as 'moisture movement'. This arises because the precise dimensions of any piece of timber are dependent on its moisture content (the ratio of the weight of water which it contains to its dry weight, expressed as a percentage). This is affected by the relative humidity of the environment and as the latter is subject to continuous change, the moisture content and therefore the dimensions of timber also fluctuate continuously. Timber shrinks following a reduction in moisture content due to decreasing relative humidity and swells if the moisture content increases. So far as the structural use of timber is concerned, one of the most serious consequences of this is that joints made with mechanical fasteners tend to work loose.

The greatest change to the moisture content of a specimen of timber occurs following the felling of a tree after which it undergoes a reduction from a value of around 150 per cent in the living tree to between 10 and 20 per cent, which is the normal range for moisture content of timber in a structure. This initial drying out causes a large amount of shrinkage and must be carried out in controlled

conditions if damage to the timber is to be avoided. The controlled drying out of timber is known as seasoning. It is a process in which the timber must be physically restrained to prevent the introduction of permanent twists and other distortions caused by the differential shrinkage which inevitably occurs, on a temporary basis, due to unevenness in the drying out. The amount of differential shrinkage must be kept to a minimum and this favours the cutting of the timber into planks with small cross-sections, because the greatest variation in moisture content occurs between timber at the core of a plank and that at the surface where evaporation of moisture takes place.

Timber elements can be either of sawn timber, which is simply timber cut directly from a tree with little further processing other than shaping and smoothing, or manufactured products, to which further processing has been applied. Important examples of the latter are laminated timber and plywood.

The forms in which sawn timber is available are, to a large extent, a consequence of the arboreal origins of the material. It is convenient to cut planks from tree trunks by sawing parallel to the trunk direction and this produces straight, parallel-sided elements with rectangular cross-sections. Basic sawn-timber components are relatively small (maximum length around 6 m and maximum cross-section around 75 mm × 250 mm) due partly to the obvious fact that the maximum sizes of cross-section and length are governed by the size of the original tree, but also to the desirability of having small cross-sections for the seasoning process. They can be combined to form larger, composite elements such as trusses with nailed, screwed or bolted connections. The scale of structural assemblies is usually modest, however, due to both the small sizes of the constituent planks and to the difficulty (already discussed) of making good structural connections with mechanical fasteners.

Timber is used in loadbearing-wall structures both as the horizontal elements in masonry buildings (see Fig. 1.13) and in all-timber configurations in which vertical timber elements are spaced close together to form wall panels (Fig. 3.6). The use of timber in skeleton frame structures (beams and columns as opposed to closely spaced joists and wall panels) is less common because the concentration of internal forces which occurs in these normally requires that a stronger material such as steel be adopted. In all cases spans are relatively small, typically 5 m for floor structures of closely spaced joists of rectangular cross-section, and 20 m for roof structures with triangulated elements. All-timber structures rarely have more than two or three storeys.

Timber products are manufactured by gluing small timber elements together in conditions of close quality control. They are intended to exploit the advantages of timber while at the same time minimising the effects of its principal disadvantages, which are variability, dimensional instability, restrictions in the sizes of individual components and anisotropic behaviour. Examples of timber products are laminated timber, composite boards such as plywood, and combinations of sawn timber and composite board (Fig. 3.7).

Laminated timber (Fig. 3.7c) is a product in which elements with large rectangular cross-sections are built up by gluing together smaller

Fig. 3.6 The all-timber house is a loadbearing wall form of construction in which all of the structural elements in the walls, floors and roof are of timber. An internal wall of closely spaced sawn-timber elements is here shown supporting the upper floor of a two-storey building. Note temporary bracing which is necessary for stability until cross-walls are inserted. (Photo: A. Macdonald)

solid timber elements of rectangular cross-section. The obvious advantage of the process is that it allows the manufacture of solid elements with much larger cross-sections than are possible in sawn timber. Very long elements are also possible because the constituent boards are jointed end-to-end by means of finger joints (Fig. 3.8). The laminating process also allows the construction of elements which are tapered or have curved

27

Fig. 3.7 The I-beam with the plywood web (b) and the laminated beam (c) are examples of manufactured timber products. These normally have better technical properties than plain sawn timber elements such as that shown in (a). The high levels of glue impregnation in manufactured beams reduce dimensional instability, and major defects, such as knots, are removed from constituent sub-elements.

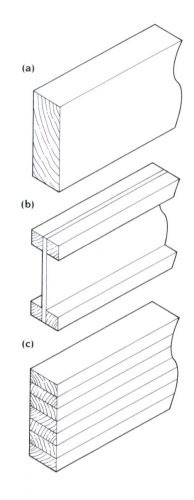

Fig. 3.9 Sports Dome, Perth, Scotland, UK. Laminated timber built-up sections can be produced in a variety of configurations in addition to straight beams. Here a series of arch elements is used to produce the framework of a dome.

profiles. Arches (Figs 3.9 and 3.10) and portal frame elements (Fig. 3.4) are examples of this.

The general quality and strength of laminated timber is higher than that of sawn timber for two principal reasons. Firstly, the use of basic components which have small cross-sections allows more effective seasoning, with fewer seasoning defects than can be achieved with large sawn-timber elements. Secondly, the use of the finger joint, which causes a minimal reduction in strength in the constituent boards, allows any major defects which are present in these to be cut out. The principal use of laminated timber is as an extension to the range of sawn-timber elements and it is employed in similar structural configurations – for example as closely spaced joists – and allows larger spans to be achieved. The higher strength of laminated timber elements also allows it to be used effectively in skeleton frame construction.

Composite boards are manufactured products composed of wood and glue. There are various types of these including plywood, blockboard and particle board, all of which are available in the form of thin sheets. The level of glue impregnation is high and this imparts good dimensional stability and reduces the

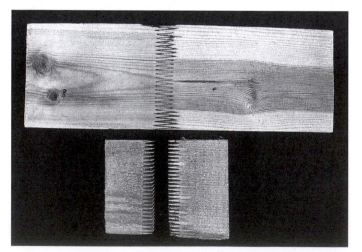

Fig. 3.8 'Finger' joints allow the constituent boards of laminated timber elements to be produced in long lengths. They also make possible the cutting out of defects such as knots. (Photo: TRADA)

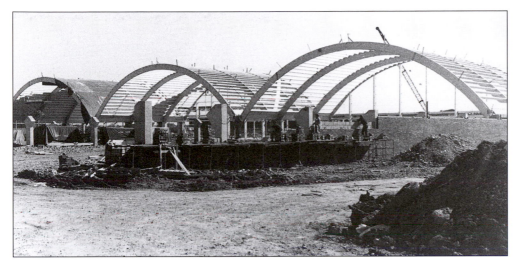

Fig. 3.10 David Lloyd Tennis Centre, London, UK. The primary structural elements are laminated timber arches which span 35 m. (Photo: TRADA)

Fig. 3.12 Sports Stadium at Lähderanta, Sweden. The primary structural elements are plywood timber arches with rectangular box cross-sections. (Photo: Finnish Plywood International)

extent to which anisotropic behaviour occurs. Most composite boards also have high resistance to splitting at areas of stress concentration around nails and screws.

Composite boards are used as secondary components such as gusset plates in built-up timber structures. Another common use is as the web elements in composite beams of I- or rectangular-box section in which the flanges are sawn timber (Figs 3.11 and 3.12).

Fig. 3.11 Built-up-beams with I-shaped cross-sections consisting of sawn timber flanges connected by a plywood web. The latter is corrugated which allows the necessary compressive stability to be achieved with a very thin cross-section. (Photo: Finnish Plywood International)

To sum up, timber is a material which offers the designers of buildings a combination of properties that allow the creation of lightweight structures which are simple to construct. However, its relatively low strength, the small sizes of the basic components and the difficulties associated with achieving good structural joints tend to limit the size of structure which is possible, and the majority of timber structures are small in scale with short spans and a small number of storeys. Currently, its most common application in architecture is in domestic building where it is used as a primary structural material either to form the entire structure of a building, as in timber wall-panel construction, or as the horizontal elements in loadbearing masonry structures.

3.4 Steel

The use of steel as a primary structural material dates from the late nineteenth century when cheap methods for manufacturing it on a large scale were developed, It is a material that has good structural properties. It has high strength and equal strength in tension and compression and is therefore suitable for the full range of structural elements and will resist axial tension, axial compression and bending-type load with almost equal facility. Its density is high, but the ratio of strength to weight is also high so that steel components are not excessively heavy in relation to their load carrying capacity, so long as structural forms are used which ensure that the material is used efficiently. Therefore, where bending loads are carried it is essential that 'improved'

Fig. 3.13 Hopkins House, London, UK; Michael Hopkins, architect; Anthony Hunt Associates, structural engineers. The floor structure here consists of profiled steel sheeting which will support a timber deck. A more common configuration is for the profiled steel deck to act compositively with an *in situ* concrete slab for which it serves as permanent formwork. (Photo: Pat Hunt)

cross-sections (see Section 4.3) and longitudinal profiles are adopted.

The high strength and high density of steel favours its use in skeleton frame type structures in which the volume of the structure is low in relation to the total volume of the building which is supported, but a limited range of slab-type formats is also used. An example of a structural slab-type element is the profiled floor deck in which a profiled steel deck is used in conjunction with concrete, or exceptionally timber (Fig. 3.13), to form a composite structure. These have 'improved' corrugated cross-sections to ensure that adequate levels of efficiency are achieved. Deck units consisting of flat steel plate are uncommon.

The shapes of steel elements are greatly influenced by the process which is used to form them. Most are shaped either by hot-rolling or by cold-forming. Hot-rolling is a primary shaping process in which massive red-hot billets of steel are rolled between several sets of profiled rollers. The cross-section of the original billet, which is normally cast from freshly manufactured steel and is usually around 0.5 m × 0.5 m square, is reduced by the rolling process to much smaller dimensions and to a particular precise shape (Fig. 3.14). The range of cross-section shapes which are produced is very large and each requires its own set of finishing rollers. Elements that are intended for structural use have shapes in which the second moment of area (see Appendix 2.3) is high in relation to the total area (Fig. 3.15). I- and H- shapes of cross-section are common for the large elements which form the beams and columns of structural frameworks. Channel and angle shapes are suitable for smaller elements such as secondary cladding supports and sub-elements in triangulated frameworks. Square, circular and rectangular hollow sections are produced in a wide range of sizes as are flat plates and solid bars of various thicknesses. Details of the dimensions and geometric properties of all the standard sections are listed in tables of section properties produced by steelwork manufacturers.

Fig. 3.14 The heaviest steel sections are produced by a hot-rolling process in which billets of steel are shaped by profiled rollers. This results in elements which are straight, parallel sided and of constant cross-section. These features must be taken into account by the designer when steel is used in building and the resulting restrictions in form accepted. (Photo: British Steel)

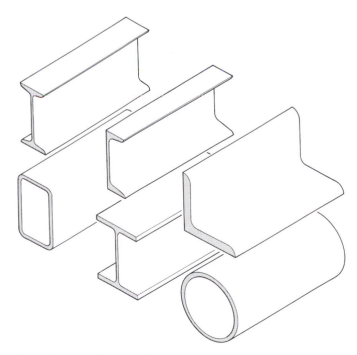

Fig. 3.15 Hot-rolled steel elements.

The other method by which large quantities of steel components are manufactured is cold-forming. In this process thin, flat sheets of steel, which have been produced by the hot-rolling process, are folded or bent in the cold state to form structural cross-sections (Fig. 3.16). The elements which result have similar characteristics to hot-rolled sections, in that they are parallel sided with constant cross-sections, but the thickness of the metal is much less so that they are both much lighter and, of course, have lower load carrying capacities. The process allows more complicated shapes of cross-section to be achieved, however. Another difference from hot-rolling is that the manufacturing equipment for cold-forming is much simpler and can be used to produce tailor-made cross-sections for specific applications. Due to their lower carrying capacities cold-formed sections are used principally for secondary elements in roof structures, such as purlins, and for cladding support systems. Their potential for future development is enormous.

Structural steel components can also be produced by casting, in which case very complex tailor-made shapes are possible. The technique is problematic when used for structural components, however, due to the difficulty of ensuring that the castings are sound and of consistent quality throughout. In the early years of ferrous metal structures in the nineteenth century, when casting was widely used, many structural failures occurred – most notably that of the Tay Railway Bridge in Scotland in 1879. The technique was rarely used for most of the twentieth century but technical advances made possible its re-introduction. Prominent recent examples are the 'gerberettes' at the Centre Pompidou, Paris (Figs 3.17 & 7.7) and the joints in the steelwork of the train shed at Waterloo Station, London (Fig. 7.17).

Most of the structural steelwork used in building consists of elements of the hot-rolled type and this has important consequences for the layout and overall form of the structures. An obvious consequence of the rolling process is that the constituent elements are prismatic: they are parallel-sided with constant cross-sections and they are straight – this tends to impose a regular, straight-sided format on the structure (see Figs iv, 1.10 and 7.26). In recent years, however, methods have been developed for bending hot-rolled structural steel elements into curved profiles and this has extended the range of forms for which steel can be used. The manufacturing process does, however, still impose quite severe restrictions on the overall shape of structure for which steel can be used.

The manufacturing process also affects the level of efficiency which can be achieved in steel structures, for several reasons. Firstly, it is not normally possible to produce specific tailor-made cross-sections for particular applications because special rolling equipment would be required to produce them and the capital cost of this would normally be well beyond the budget of an individual project. Standard sections must normally be adopted in the interests of economy, and efficiency is compromised as a result. An alternative is the use of tailor-made elements built up by welding together standard components, such as I-sections built up from flat plate. This involves higher manufacturing costs than the use of standard rolled sections.

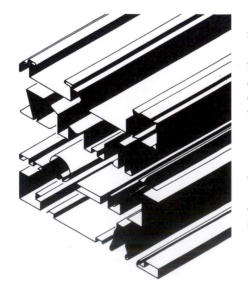

Fig. 3.16 Cold-formed sections are formed from thin steel sheet. A greater variety of cross-section shapes is possible than with the hot-rolling process.

(a)

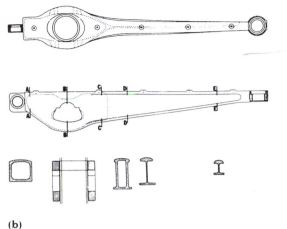

(b)

Fig. 3.17 The so-called 'gerberettes' at the Centre Pompidou in Paris, France, are cast steel components. No other process could have produced elements of this size and shape in steel. (Photo: A. Macdonald)

A second disadvantage of using an 'off-the-peg' item is that the standard section has a constant cross-section and therefore constant strength along its length. Most structural elements are subjected to internal forces which vary from cross-section to cross-section and therefore have a requirement for varying strength along their length. It is, of course, possible to vary the size of cross-section which is provided to a limited extent. The depth of an I-section element, for example, can be varied by cutting one or both flanges from the web, cutting the web to a tapered profile and then welding the flanges back on again. The same type of tapered I-beam can also be produced by welding together three separate flat plates to form an I-shaped cross-section, as described above.

Because steel structures are pre-fabricated, the design of the joints between the elements is an important aspect of the overall design which affects both the structural performance and the appearance of the frame. Joints are made either by bolting or by welding (Fig. 3.18). Bolted joints are less effective for the transmission of load because bolt holes reduce the effective sizes of element cross-sections and give rise to stress concentrations. Bolted connections can also be unsightly unless carefully detailed. Welded joints are neater and transmit load more effectively, but the welding process is a highly skilled operation and requires that the components concerned be very carefully prepared and precisely aligned prior to the joint being made. For these reasons welding on building sites is normally avoided and steel structures are normally pre-fabricated by welding and bolted together on site. The need to transport elements to the site restricts both the size and shape of individual components.

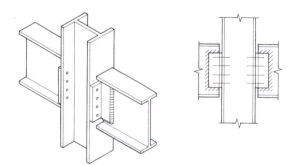

Fig. 3.18 Joints in steelwork are normally made by a combination of bolting and welding. The welding is usually carried out in the fabricating workshop and the site joint is made by bolting.

Fig. 3.19 Renault Sales Headquarters, Swindon, UK, 1983; Foster Associates, architects; Ove Arup & Partners, structural engineers. Joints in steelwork can be detailed to look very neat and to convey a feeling of great precision. (Photo: Alastair Hunter)

Steel is manufactured in conditions of very high quality control and therefore has dependable properties which allow the use of low factors of safety in structural design. This, together with its high strength, results in slender elements of lightweight appearance. The basic shapes of both hot- and cold-formed components are controlled within small tolerances and the metal lends itself to very fine machining and welding with the result that joints of neat appearance can be made. The overall visual effect is of a structure which has been made with great precision (Fig. 3.19).

Two problems associated with steel are its poor performance in fire, due to the loss of mechanical properties at relatively low temperatures, and its high chemical instability, which makes it susceptible to corrosion. Both of these have been overcome to some extent by the development of fireproof and corrosion protection materials, especially paints, but the exposure of steel structures, either internally, where fire must be considered, or externally, where durability is an issue, is always problematic.

To sum up, steel is a very strong material with dependable properties. It is used principally in skeleton frame types of structure in which the components are hot-rolled. It allows the production of structures of a light, slender appearance and a feeling of neatness and high precision. It is also capable of producing very long span structures, and structures of great height. The manufacturing process imposes certain restrictions on the forms of steel frames. Regular overall shapes produced from straight, parallel-sided elements are the most favoured.

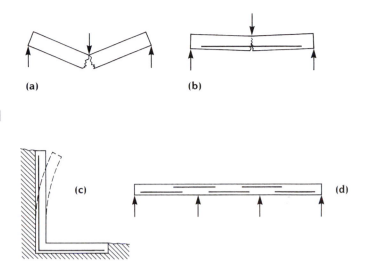

3.5 Concrete

Concrete, which is a composite of stone fragments (aggregate) and cement binder, may be regarded as a kind of artificial masonry because it has similar properties to stone and brick (high density, moderate compressive strength, minimal tensile strength). It is made by mixing together dry cement and aggregate in suitable proportions and then adding water, which causes the cement to hydrolyse and subsequently the whole mixture to set and harden to form a substance with stone-like qualities.

Plain, unreinforced concrete has similar properties to masonry and so the constraints on its use are the same as those which apply to masonry, and which were outlined in Section 3.2. The most spectacular plain concrete structures are also the earliest – the massive vaulted buildings of Roman antiquity (see Figs 7.30 to 7.32).

Concrete has one considerable advantage over stone, which is that it is available in semi-liquid form during the building process and this has three important consequences. Firstly, it means that other materials can be incorporated into it easily to augment its properties. The most important of these is steel in the form of thin reinforcing bars which give the resulting composite material (reinforced concrete) (Fig. 3.20) tensile and therefore bending strength as well as compressive strength. Secondly, the availability of concrete in liquid form allows it to be cast into a wide variety of shapes. Thirdly, the casting process allows very effective connections to be provided between elements and the resulting structural continuity greatly enhances the efficiency of the structure (see Appendix 3).

Reinforced concrete possesses tensile as well as compressive strength and is therefore

Fig. 3.20 In reinforced concrete, steel reinforcing bars are positioned in locations where tensile stress occurs.

suitable for all types of structural element including those which carry bending-type loads. It is also a reasonably strong material. Concrete can therefore be used in structural configurations such as the skeleton frame for which a strong material is required and the resulting elements are reasonably slender. It can also be used to make long-span structures and high, multi-storey structures.

Although concrete can be moulded into complicated shapes, relatively simple shapes are normally favoured for reasons of economy in construction (Fig. 3.21). The majority of

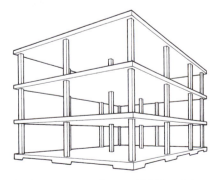

Fig. 3.21 Despite the mouldability of the material, reinforced concrete structures normally have a relatively simple form so as to economise on construction costs. A typical arrangement for a multi-storey framework is shown.

reinforced concrete structures are therefore post-and-beam arrangements (see Section 5.2) of straight beams and columns, with simple solid rectangular or circular cross-sections, supporting plane slabs of constant thickness. The formwork in which such structures are cast is simple to make and assemble and therefore inexpensive, and can be re-used repeatedly in the same building. These non-form-active arrangements (see Section 4.2) are relatively inefficient but are satisfactory where the spans are short (up to 6 m). Where longer spans are required more efficient 'improved' types of cross-section (see Section 4.3) and profile are adopted. The range of possibilities is large due to the mouldability of the material. Commonly used examples are coffered slabs and tapered beam profiles.

The mouldability of concrete also makes possible the use of complex shapes and the inherent properties of the material are such that practically any shape is possible. Reinforced concrete has therefore been used for a very wide range of structural geometries. Examples of structures in which this has been exploited are the Willis, Faber and Dumas building (see Fig. 7.37), where the mouldability of concrete and the level of structural continuity which it makes possible were used to produce a multi-storey structure of irregularly curved plan with floors which

cantilevered beyond the perimeter columns, and the Lloyd's Building, in London (Fig. 7.9), in which an exposed concrete frame was given great prominence and detailed to express the structural nature of its function. The buildings of Richard Meier (see Fig. 1.9) and Peter Eisenman (see Fig. 5.18) are also examples of structures in which the innate properties of reinforced concrete have been well exploited.

Sometimes the geometries which are adopted for concrete structures are selected for their high efficiency. Form-active shells for which reinforced concrete is ideally suited are examples of this (see Fig. 1.4). The efficiency of these is very high and spans of 100 m and more have been achieved with shells a few tens of millimetres in thickness. In other cases the high levels of structural continuity have made possible the creation of sculptured building forms which, though they may be expressive of architectural meanings, are not particularly sensible from a structural point of view. A well-known example of this is the roof of the chapel at Ronchamp (see Fig. 7.40) by Le Corbusier, in which a highly individual and inefficient structural form is executed in reinforced concrete. Another example is the Vitra Design Museum by Frank Gehry (see Fig. 7.41). It would have been impossible to make these forms in any other structural material.

Chapter 4

The relationship between structural form and structural efficiency

4.1 Introduction

This chapter is concerned with the relationship between structural form and structural performance. In particular, the effect of structural geometry on the efficiency[1] with which particular levels of strength and rigidity can be achieved is explored.

The shapes of structural elements, especially the shapes of their longitudinal axes in relation to the pattern of applied load, determine the types of internal force which occur within them and influence the magnitudes of these forces. These two factors – the type and the magnitude of the internal force created by a given application of load – have a marked effect on the level of structural efficiency which can be achieved because they determine the amount of material which must be provided to give the elements adequate strength and rigidity.

A classification system for structural elements is proposed here based on the relationship between form and efficiency. Its purpose is to aid the understanding of the role of structural elements in determining the performance of complete structures. It therefore provides a basis for the reading of a building as a structural object.

---

[1] Structural efficiency is considered here in terms of the weight of material which has to be provided to carry a given amount of load. The efficiency of an element is regarded as high if the ratio of its strength to its weight is high.

4.2 The effect of form on internal force type

Elements in architectural structures are subjected principally either to axial internal force or to bending-type internal force. They may also be subjected to a combination of these. The distinction between axial and bending is an important one, so far as efficiency is concerned, because axial internal force can be resisted more efficiently than bending-type internal force. The principal reason for this is that the distribution of stress which occurs within the cross-sections of axially loaded elements is more or less constant, and this uniform level of stress allows all of the material in the element to be stressed to its limit. A size of cross-section is selected which ensures that the level of stress is as high as the material concerned can safely withstand and an efficient use of material therefore results because all of the material present provides full value for its weight. With bending stress, which varies in intensity in all cross-sections (Fig. 4.1) from a minimum at the neutral axis to a maximum at the extreme fibres (see Appendix 2), only the material at the extreme fibres can be stressed to its limit. Most of the material present is understressed and therefore inefficiently used.

The type of internal force which occurs in an element depends on the relationship between the direction of its principal axis (its longitudinal axis) and the direction of the load which is applied to it (Fig. 4.2). If an element is straight, axial internal force occurs if the load is applied parallel to the longitudinal axis of the element. Bending-type internal force occurs if it is applied at right angles to the longitudinal

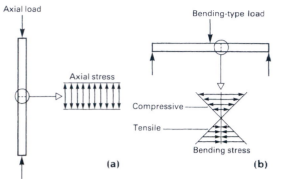

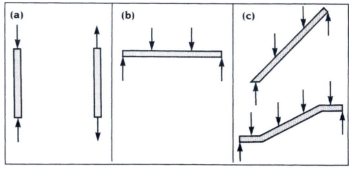

Fig. 4.1 (a) Elements which carry purely axial load are subjected to axial stress whose intensity is constant across all cross-sectional planes. (b) Pure bending-type load (i.e. load which is normal to the axis of the element) causes bending stress to occur on all cross-sectional planes. The magnitude of this varies within each cross-section from a maximum compressive stress at one extremity to a maximum tensile stress at the other.

Fig. 4.2 Basic relationships between loads and structural elements. (a) Load coincident with principal axis; axial internal force. (b) Load perpendicular to the principal axis; bending-type internal force. (c) Load inclined to the principal axis; combined axial and bending-type internal force.

axis. If the load is applied obliquely, a combination of axial and bending stress occurs. The axial-only and bending-only cases are in fact special cases of the more general combined case, but they are nevertheless the most commonly found types of loading arrangement in architectural structures.

If an element is not straight, it will almost inevitably be subjected to a combination of axial and bending internal forces when a load is applied, but there are important exceptions to this as is illustrated in Fig. 4.3. Here, the structural element consists of a flexible cable, supported at its ends, and from which various loads are suspended. Because the cable has no rigidity it is incapable of carrying any other type of internal force but axial tension; it is therefore forced by the loads into a shape which allows it to resist the loads with an internal force which is pure axial tension. The shape traced by the longitudinal axis is unique to the load pattern and is called the 'form-active'[2] shape for that load.

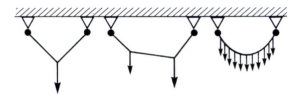

Fig. 4.3 Tensile form-active shapes. Because it has no rigidity a cable must take up a shape – the form-active shape – which allows it to resist the load with a purely tensile internal force. Different load arrangements produce different form-active shapes.

As is seen in Fig. 4.3 the shape which the cable adopts is dependent on the pattern of load which is applied; the form-active shape is straight-sided when the loads are concentrated at individual points and curved if the load is distributed along it. If a cable is allowed simply to sag under its own weight, which is a distributed load acting along its entire length, it adopts a curve known as a 'catenary' (Fig. 4.3).

An interesting feature of the form-active shape for any load pattern is that if a rigid element is constructed whose longitudinal axis is the mirror image of the form-active shape taken up by the cable, then it too will be subjected exclusively to axial internal forces when the same load is applied, despite the fact that, being rigid, it could also carry a bending-type internal force. In the mirror-image form all the axial internal forces are compressive (Fig. 4.4).

---

2 'Form-active' is a term applied by Engel in his book *Structure Systems*, 1967, to a structural element in which the shape of the longitudinal axis, in relation to the pattern of applied load, is such that the internal force is axial.

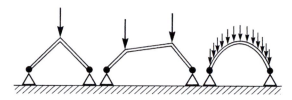

Fig. 4.4 Compressive form-active shapes.

The cable structure and its rigid 'mirror image' counterpart are simple examples of a whole class of structural elements which carry axial internal forces because their longitudinal axes conform to the form-active shapes for the loads which are applied to them. These are called 'form-active' elements.

If, in a real structure, a flexible material such as steel wire or cable is used to make an element, it will automatically take up the form-active shape when load is applied. Flexible material is in fact incapable of becoming anything other than a form-active element. If the material is rigid, however, and a form-active element is required, then it must be made to conform to the form-active shape for the load which is to be applied to it or, in the case of a compressive element, to the mirror image of the form-active shape. If not, the internal force will not be pure axial force and some bending will occur.

Figure 4.5 shows a mixture of form-active and non-form-active shapes. Two load patterns

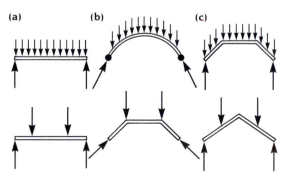

Fig. 4.5 Examples of the relationship between element shape, load pattern and element type. The latter is determined by the relationship between the shape of the element and the form-active shape for the load pattern which it carries. (a) Non-form-active (bending stress only). (b) Form-active (axial stress only). (c) Semi-form-active (combined bending and axial stress).

are illustrated: a uniformly distributed load across the whole of the element and two concentrated loads applied at equal distances across them. For each load, elements (a) carry pure bending-type internal forces; no axial force can occur in these because there is no component of either load which is parallel to the axis of the element. The elements in (b) have shapes which conform exactly to the form-active shapes of the loads. They are therefore form-active elements which carry axial internal forces only; in both cases the forces are compressive. The elements (c) do not conform to the form-active shapes for the loads and will not therefore carry pure axial internal force. Neither will they be subjected to pure bending; they will carry a combination of bending and axial internal force.

So far as the shape of their longitudinal axes are concerned, structural elements can thus be classified into three categories: form-active elements, non-form-active elements and semi-form-active elements. Form-active elements are those which conform to the form-active shape of the load pattern which is applied to them and they contain axial internal forces only. Non-form-active elements are those whose longitudinal axis does not conform to the form-active shape of the loads and is such that no axial component of internal force occurs. These contain bending-type internal force only. Semi-form-active elements are elements whose shapes are such that they contain a combination of bending and axial internal forces.

It is important to note that structural elements can only be form-active in the context of a particular load pattern. There are no shapes which are form-active *per se*. The cranked beam shape in Fig. 4.5, for example, is a fully form-active element when subjected to the two concentrated loads, but a semi-form-active element when subjected to the uniformly distributed load.

Form-active shapes are potentially the most efficient types of structural element and non-form-active shapes the least efficient. The efficiency of semi-form-active elements depends on the extent to which they are different from the form-active shape.

4.3 The concept of 'improved' shapes in cross-section and longitudinal profile

It will be remembered from the beginning of Section 4.2 that the main reason for the low efficiency of elements in which bending-type internal forces occur is the uneven distribution of stress which exists within every cross-section. This causes the material in the centre of the cross-section, adjacent to the neutral axis (see Appendix 2), to be under-stressed and therefore inefficiently used. The efficiency of an element can be improved if some of the under-stressed material is removed and this

can be achieved by a judicious choice of geometry in both cross-section and longitudinal profile.

Compare the cross-sections of Fig. 4.6 with the diagram of bending stress distribution. Most of the material in the solid rectangular cross-section is under-stressed; the load is actually carried principally by the material in the high stress regions of the cross-section which occur at its top and bottom extremities (the extreme fibres). In the I- and box-shaped cross-sections most of the under-stressed material is eliminated; the strength of elements which are given these cross-sections is almost as great as that of an element with a solid rectangular cross-section of the same overall dimensions; they contain significantly less material and are therefore lighter and more efficient.

A similar situation exists with slab-type elements. Solid slabs are much less efficient in their use of material than those in which material is removed from the interior, as can be demonstrated by carrying out a simple experiment with card (Fig. 4.7). A flat piece of thin card has a very low bending strength. If the card is arranged into a folded or corrugated geometry the bending strength is greatly increased. The card with the folded or corrugated cross-section has a strength which is equivalent to that of a solid card with the same total depth; it is, however, much lighter and therefore more efficient.

In general, cross-sections in which material is located away from the centre are more efficient in carrying bending-type loads than solid cross-sections. Solid cross-sections are, of course, much simpler to make and for this reason have an important place in the field of architectural structures, but they are poor performers compared to the I- or box-shaped cross-section so far as structural efficiency is concerned. In the classification which will be proposed here, these two categories of cross-section are referred to as 'simple solid' and 'improved' cross-sections.

The shape of an element in longitudinal profile can be manipulated in a similar way to its cross-section to improve its performance in

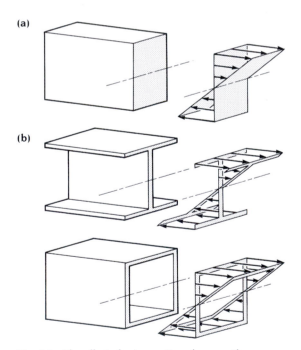

(a)

(b)

Fig. 4.6 The effect of cross-section shape on the efficiency of elements which carry bending-type loads. (a) In an element with a rectangular cross-section, high bending stress occurs at the extreme fibres only. Most of the material carries a low stress and is therefore inefficiently used. (b) In 'improved' cross-sections efficiency is increased by elimination of most of the understressed material adjacent to the centre of the cross-section.

(a)

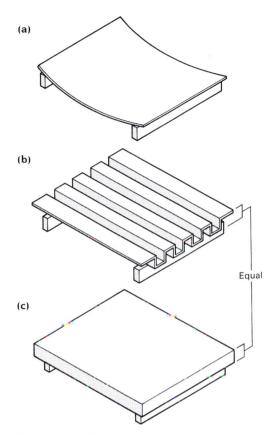

(b)

Equal

(c)

Fig. 4.7 The effect of cross-sectional shape on the efficiency with which bending-type load is resisted. (a) Thin card which has an inefficient rectangular cross-section. (b) Thin card folded to give an efficient 'improved' cross-section. (c) Thick card with inefficient rectangular cross-section and having equivalent strength and stiffness to the folded thin card.

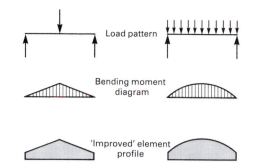

Load pattern

Bending moment diagram

'Improved' element profile

Fig. 4.8 The efficiency of a non-form-active element can be improved if its longitudinal profile is adjusted to conform to the bending moment diagram so that high strength is provided only where the internal force is high.

resisting bending-type loads. The adjustment can take the form of alteration to the overall shape of the profile or to its internal geometry.

To improve efficiency the overall shape is adjusted by varying the depth of the element: this is the dimension on which bending strength principally depends (see Appendix 2). If the depth is varied according to the intensity of bending (specifically to the magnitude of the bending moment) then a more efficient use of material is achieved than if a constant depth of cross-section is used. Figure 4.8 shows two beam profiles which have been improved in this way. They are deep at the locations where

the bending moment is high and shallow where it is low.

The internal geometry of the longitudinal profile can also be improved by altering it to remove under-stressed material from the interior of the element. Examples of elements in which this has been done are shown in Fig. 4.9. As in the case of cross-sectional shape the internal geometry of the longitudinal profile of an element will be referred to here as 'simple solid' or 'improved'.

One type of 'improved' profile which is of great importance in architectural as well as all other types of structure is the triangulated profile (i.e. the profile which consists entirely of triangles) (Fig. 4.10). If an element of this type has loads applied to it at the vertices of the triangles only, then the individual sub-elements which form the triangles are

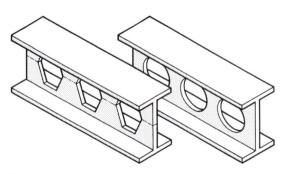

Fig. 4.9 The efficiency of non-form-active elements can be improved by selecting a shape in longitudinal profile in which material is removed from the understressed centre of the element.

41

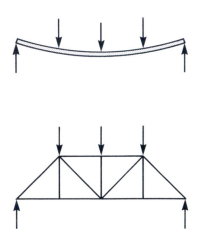

Fig. 4.11 An alteration of the geometry of a triangle can only occur if the length of one of the sides changes. Application of load to a triangle, which tends to distort its geometry, is therefore resisted by axial internal forces in the elements.

Fig. 4.10 A solid beam is less strong and rigid than a triangulated structure of equivalent weight.

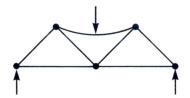

Fig. 4.12 The axial-internal-force-only condition does not occur if load is applied to a triangulated structure other than at its joints.

subjected to axial internal forces only[3] (Figs 4.11 and 4.12). This applies no matter what the relationship is between the pattern of loads and the longitudinal axis of the element, taken as a whole.

By eliminating bending stress from non-form-active elements the triangulated internal geometry allows a high degree of structural efficiency to be achieved. The advantage of the triangulated element over the other class of element for which this is true – the form-active element – is that no special overall form is

required to produce the axial-stress-only condition. All that is required is that the internal geometry be fully triangulated and the external load applied only at the joints. Triangulated elements do not, however, achieve quite such a high degree of structural efficiency as form-active structures due to the relatively high level of internal force which occurs.

Certain bending-type elements with 'improved' cross-sections are referred to as 'stressed skin', 'monocoque' or 'semi-monocoque' elements to distinguish them from skeletal elements which consist of a framework of structural sub-elements covered by non-structural skin. The distinction is perhaps best seen in the field of aeronautical engineering by comparison of the structure of a fabric-covered 'stick-and-string' biplane with that of an all-metal aircraft (Fig. 4.13). In each case the fuselage is a structure which carries bending as well as other types of internal force, notably torsion. Aircraft structures must, of course, have a very high ratio of strength to weight. Form-active or semi-form-active arrangements are impractical, however,

---

3 This property is a consequence of a characteristic unique to the triangle among geometric figures, which is that its geometry can only be changed if the length of one or more of its sides is altered. (The geometry of any other polygon can be changed by altering the angles between the sides and maintaining the sides at a constant length – Fig. 4.11.) The resistance which is generated by a triangulated structure to a potential alteration in geometry (which is what occurs when a load is applied) takes the form of a resistance to change in length of the sides of the triangles. This results in the sub-elements which form the sides of the triangles being placed into either axial tension or axial compression. The axial-stress-only state therefore occurs no matter what the overall form of the element, provided that its internal geometry is fully triangulated with straight-sided triangles and the load is applied only to the joints between the sub-elements. If a load is applied directly to one of the constituent sub-elements and not at a joint, as in Fig. 4.12, then bending will occur in that sub-element.

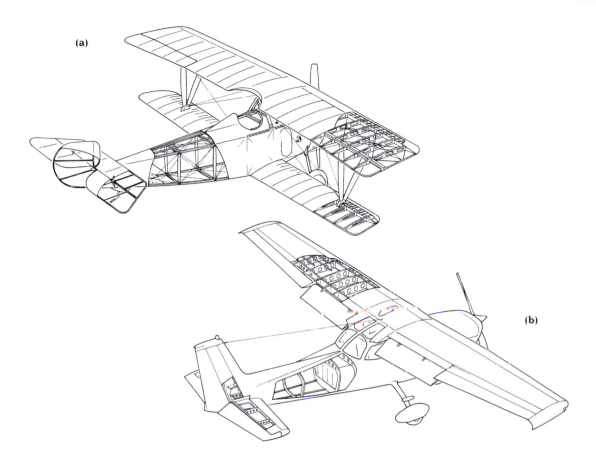

(a)

(b)

Fig. 4.13 The overall shapes of aircraft are determined mainly from non-structural considerations, principally aerodynamic performance requirements. The supporting structures are therefore non-form-active, but the very high priority which must be given to saving of weight results in the adoption of configurations in which many 'improvements' are incorporated. (a) The fuselage and wings of the 'stick-and-string' biplane have triangulated structures of timber and wire. The fabric covering has a minimal structural function. (b) The wings and fuselage of the all-metal aircraft are hollow box-beams in which the skin plays an essential structural role.

because the overall shapes of aircraft are determined from aerodynamic rather than structural considerations. The structures are therefore non-form-active and must have 'improved' internal structures so as to meet the required levels of efficiency.

In the case of the early biplane fuselage the fabric skin had virtually no structural function and the loads were carried entirely by the framework of timber and wire which, being

fully triangulated, was an efficient type of structure with a high ratio of strength to weight. Its disadvantage was that its potential strength was limited firstly by the relative weakness of timber, and secondly by the difficulty of making efficient joints between the timber compressive elements and the wire tensile elements. As the size and speed of aircraft increased and stronger aircraft structures were required, the change to an all-metal structure became inevitable. The fabric skin was replaced by sheeting of aluminium alloy and the internal structure of timber and wire by ribs and longitudinal stringers also of aluminium alloy. In this more sophisticated type of aircraft structure, which is called a semi-monocoque structure, the metal skin acted with the ribs and stringers to form a composite structure called a 'stressed-skin semi-monocoque'. Monocoque construction is the term used where the element consists only of the stressed skin.

43

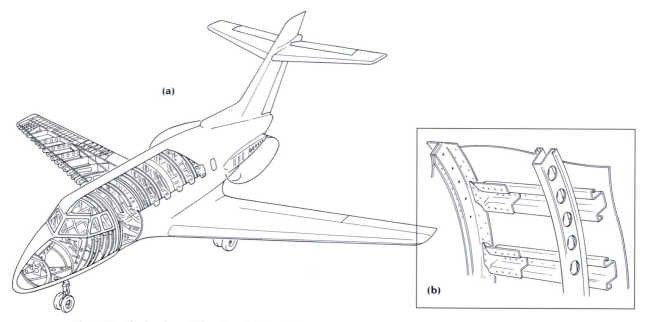

Fig. 4.14 The fuselage of the all-metal aircraft is a non-form-active structure which is 'improved' at various levels. The fuselage, taken as a whole, is a hollow box-beam. 'Improvements' of several types are incorporated into the sub-elements which support the structural skin.

In the semi-monocoque fuselage of an all-metal aircraft (Fig. 4.14), which is a non-form-active structural element with an 'improved' cross-section, a very thin stressed skin is used which must be strengthened at regular intervals by ribs and stringers to prevent local buckling from occurring. The technique of improvement may be seen to be operating at several levels. The fuselage, taken as a whole, is a non-form-active element with an 'improved' hollow-tube cross-section. Further 'improvement' occurs in the tube walls, which have a complex cross-section consisting of the stressed skin acting in conjunction with the strengthening ribs and stringers. These strengthening sub-elements are in turn 'improved' by having cross-sections of complex shape and circular holes cut in their webs.

The all-metal aircraft structure is therefore a complicated assembly of sub-elements to which the technique of 'improvement' has been applied at several levels. The complexity results in a structure which is efficient but which is very costly to produce. This is justified in the interests of saving weight. Every kilonewton saved contributes to the performance of the aircraft so weight saving is allocated a very high priority in the design.

A similar application of the features which save weight can be seen in the field of vehicle design, especially railway carriages and motor cars. The structure of the modern railway carriage consists of a metal tube which forms its skin, spanning as a beam between the bogies on which it is mounted. It is a non-form-active 'improved' box beam. The structure of a motor car is similar: the steel car body acts as a beam to carry the weight of the engine, occupants, etc. between the road wheels (Fig. 4.15). As in the case of the aeroplane the overall forms of rail and road vehicles are determined largely from non-structural considerations, but the need to save weight is given a high priority in the design. Again the use of 'improved' non-form-active monocoque and semi-monocoque structures constitutes a sensible response to the technical problems posed.

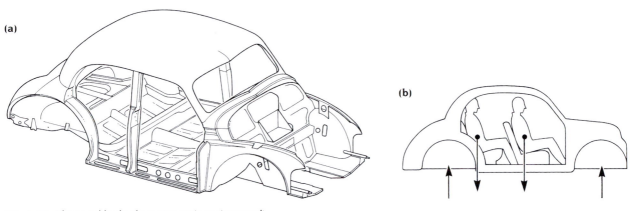

(a)

(b)

Fig. 4.15 The metal body of a motor car is an 'improved' non-form-active beam which spans between the road wheels.

The use of such elaborate forms of 'improvement' as the monocoque or semi-monocoque stressed skin can rarely be justified on technical grounds in architectural structures because the saving of weight is not a sufficiently high priority to justify the expense of this complex type of structure. In the case of buildings, inefficient high-mass structures can actually be advantageous. They add thermal mass and their weight counteracts wind uplift.

The uses of the devices and configurations which produce efficient and therefore lightweight structures – the complex cross-section, the circular 'lightening' hole, triangulation of elements and profiling to conform to bending moment diagrams – are not always appropriate from the technical viewpoint in the context of architecture where they are justified technically only in situations in which an efficient, lightweight structure is required (see Chapter 6). They can, however, have another architectural function which is to form a visual vocabulary of structure.

The use of the devices associated with structural efficiency for stylistic purposes is discussed in Chapter 7. It might be observed here that where this occurs they are often used in situations which are inappropriate structurally. The devices of 'improvement' which were devised in the context of aeronautical and vehicle engineering have become, in the hands of modern architects, especially those of 'high-tech' architects, a visual version of the dead metaphor.

4.4 Classification of structural elements

The principles outlined in the preceding sections, concerned with the various devices which can be used to improve the efficiency of structures, can form the basis of a classification system for structural elements. This is illustrated in Table 4.1. The primary categorisation is between form-active, semi-form-active and non-form-active elements because this is the most important factor in determining the level of efficiency which can be achieved. Elements are further classified according to the degree of 'improvement' which is present in their cross-sections and longitudinal profiles. The number of combinations and permutations is very large and a selection only of possibilities is illustrated in Table 4.1 to show the general principles involved. The least efficient shapes (non-form-active elements with simple shapes in both cross-section and longitudinal profile) are placed at the top of the table and the degree of efficiency present increases towards the bottom of the table, where the most efficient shapes – tensile form-active elements – are placed. A distinction is made between line elements,

45

Table 4.1

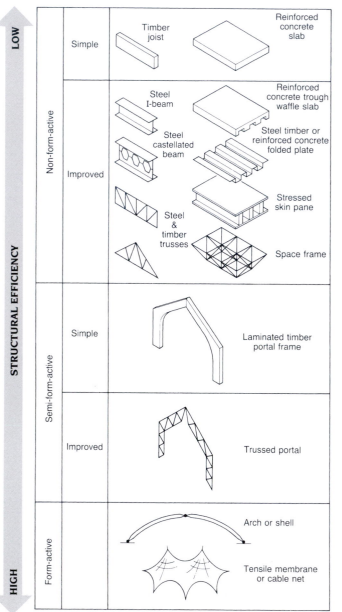

such as beams, in which one dimension is significantly larger than the other two, and surface elements, such as slabs, in which one dimension is significantly smaller than the other two.

This system links the form, and therefore the appearance, of a structure with its technical performance and provides a basis for reading a building, or indeed any artefact, as a structural object. This is an important consideration for anyone involved with either the design of buildings or with their critical appraisal.

The system is based on the idea of efficiency: structural elements are classified according to the level of efficiency which they make possible in the resistance of load which is, of course, their principal function. The main objective of structural design, however, is the achievement of an appropriate level of efficiency rather than the maximum possible level of efficiency. The factors which determine the level of efficiency which is appropriate are discussed in Chapter 6. The discussion of whether or not an appropriate level of efficiency has been achieved cannot take place, however, in the absence of a means of judging efficiency. The system proposed here provides that means.

An aspect of the relationship between structure and architecture which has been touched on in this chapter is the possibility that the features associated with structural efficiency can be used as the basis of a visual vocabulary which conveys architectural meaning – the message being technical progress and excellence. This issue is discussed in Section 7.2.2.

Chapter 5

Complete structural arrangements

5.1 Introduction

Most structures are assemblies of large numbers of elements and the performance of the complete structure depends principally on the types of element which it contains and on the ways in which these are connected together. The classification of elements was considered in Chapter 4, where the principal influence on element type was shown to be the shape of the element in relation to the pattern of the applied load. In the context of architecture, where gravitational loads are normally paramount, there are three basic arrangements: post-and-beam, form-active and semi-form-active (Fig. 5.1). Post-and-beam structures are assemblies of vertical and horizontal elements (the latter being non-form-active); fully form-active structures are

complete structures whose geometries conform to the form-active shape for the principal load which is applied; arrangements which do not fall into either of these categories are semi-form-active.

The nature of the joints between elements (be they form-active, semi-form-active or non-form-active) significantly affects the performance of structures and by this criterion they are said to be either 'discontinuous' or 'continuous' depending on how the elements are connected. Discontinuous structures contain only sufficient constraints to render them stable; they are assemblies of elements connected together by hinge-type joints[1] and most of them are also statically determinate (see Appendix 3). Typical examples are shown diagrammatically in Fig. 5.2. Continuous structures, the majority of which are also statically indeterminate (see Appendix 3), contain more than the minimum number of constraints required for stability. They usually have very few hinge-type joints and many have none at all (Fig. 5.3). Most structural geometries can be made either continuous or discontinuous depending on the nature of the connections between the elements.

The principal merit of the discontinuous structure is that it is simple, both to design and to construct. Other advantages are that its behaviour in response to differential settlement of the foundations and to changes in the lengths of elements, such as occur

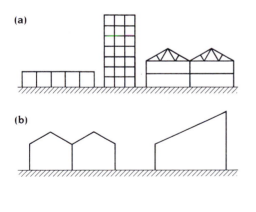

(a)

(b)

(c)

Fig. 5.1 The three categories of basic geometry. (a) Post-and-beam. (b) Semi-form-active. (c) Form-active.

---

1   A hinge joint is not literally a hinge; it is simply a joint which is incapable of preventing elements from rotating relative to each other; most junctions between elements fall into this category.

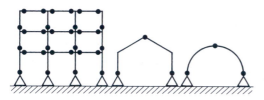

Fig. 5.2 Discontinuous structures. The multi-storey frame has insufficient constraints for stability and would require the addition of a bracing system. The three-hinge portal frame and three-hinge arch are self-bracing, statically determinate structures.

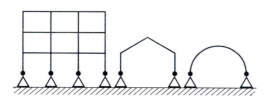

Fig. 5.3 Continuous structures. All are self-bracing and statically indeterminate.

when they expand or contract due to variations in temperature, does not give rise to additional stress. The discontinuous structure adjusts its geometry in these circumstances to accommodate the movement without any internal force being introduced into the elements. A disadvantage of the discontinuous structure is that, for a given application of load, it contains larger internal forces than a continuous structure with the same basic geometry; larger elements are required to achieve the same load carrying capacity and it is therefore less efficient. A further disadvantage is that it must normally be given a more regular geometry than an equivalent continuous structure in order that it can be geometrically stable. This restricts the freedom of the designer in the selection of the form which is adopted and obviously affects the shape of the building which can be supported. The regular geometry of typical steel frameworks, many of which are discontinuous (see Figs 2.11 and 5.16) illustrate this. The discontinuous structure is therefore a rather basic structural arrangement which is not very efficient but which is simple and therefore economical to design and construct.

The behaviour of continuous structures is altogether more complex than that of discontinuous forms. They are more difficult both to design and to construct (see Appendix 3) and they are also unable to accommodate movements such as thermal expansion and foundation settlement without the creation of internal forces which are additional to those caused by the loads. They are nevertheless potentially more efficient than discontinuous structures and have a greater degree of geometric stability. These properties allow the designer greater freedom to manipulate the overall form of the structure and therefore of the building which it supports. Figures 1.9 and 7.37 show buildings with continuous structures which illustrate this point.

5.2 Post-and-beam structures

Post-and-beam structures are either loadbearing wall structures or frame structures. Both are commonly used structural forms and within each type a fairly wide variety of different structural arrangements, of both the continuous and the discontinuous types, are possible. A large range of spans is also possible depending on the types of element which are used.

The loadbearing wall structure is a post-and-beam arrangement in which a series of horizontal elements is supported on vertical walls (Fig. 5.4). If, as is usually the case, the joints between the elements are of the hinge type, the horizontal elements are subjected to pure bending-type internal forces and the vertical elements to pure axial compressive internal forces when gravitational loads are applied. The basic form is unstable but stability is provided by bracing walls, and the plans of these buildings therefore consist of two sets of walls: loadbearing walls and bracing walls (Fig. 5.5). The loadbearing walls, which carry the weights of the floors and roof, are usually positioned more or less parallel to one another at approximately equally spaced and as close together as space-planning requirements will allow in order to minimise

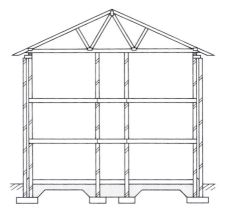

Fig. 5.4 In the cross-section of a post-and-beam loadbearing masonry structure the reinforced concrete floors at the first- and second-storey levels span one way between the outer walls and central spine walls. Timber trussed rafters carry the roof and span across the whole building between the outer walls.

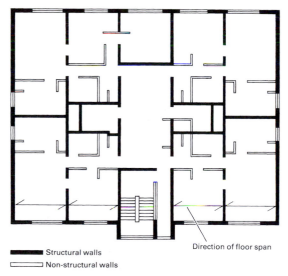

■■■ Structural walls
▭ Non-structural walls

Direction of floor span

Fig. 5.5 Typical plan of a multi-storey loadbearing wall structure. The floor structure spans one way between parallel structural walls. Selected walls in the orthogonal direction act as bracing elements.

the spans. The bracing walls are normally run in a perpendicular direction and the interiors of the buildings are therefore multi-cellular and rectilinear in plan. Irregular plan forms are possible, however. In multi-storey versions the plan must be more or less the same at every level so as to maintain vertical continuity of the loadbearing walls.

Loadbearing wall structures are used for a wide range of building types and sizes of building (Figs 5.6, 1.13 and 7.36). The smallest are domestic types of one or two storeys in which the floors and roofs are normally of timber and the walls of either timber or masonry. In all-timber construction (see Fig. 3.6), the walls are composed of closely spaced columns tied together at the base and head of the walls to form panels, and the floors are similarly constructed. Where the walls are of masonry, the floors can be of timber or reinforced concrete. The latter are heavier but they have the advantage of being able to span in two directions simultaneously. This allows the adoption of more irregular arrangements of supporting walls and generally increases planning freedom (Fig. 5.7). Reinforced concrete floors are also capable of larger spans than are timber floors; they provide buildings which are stronger and more stable and have the added advantage of providing a fireproof structure.

Although beams and slabs with simple, solid cross-sections are normally used for the floor elements of loadbearing-wall buildings, because the spans are usually short (see Section 6.2), axially stressed elements in the form of triangulated trusses are frequently used to form the horizontal elements in the roof structures. The most commonly used lightweight roof elements are timber trusses (Fig. 5.8) and lightweight steel lattice girders.

The discontinuous loadbearing wall configuration is a very basic form of structure in which the most elementary types of bending (i.e. non-form-active) elements, with simple, solid cross-sections, are employed. Their efficiency is low and a further disadvantage is that the requirements of the structure impose fairly severe restrictions on the freedom of the designer to plan the form of the building – the primary constraints being the need to adopt a multi-cellular interior in which none of the spaces is very large and, in multi-storey buildings, a plan which is more or less the same at every level. The structures are straightforward and economical to construct, however.

Fig. 5.6 Corinthian Court, Abingdon, UK; the Baron Willmore Partnership, architects; Glanville and Associates, structural engineers. The vertical structure of this three-storey office building, which measures 55 m by 20 m on plan and has few internal walls, is of loadbearing masonry. The floors are of reinforced concrete.

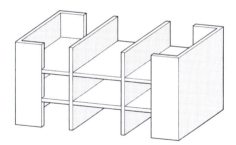

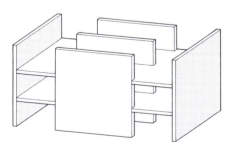

Fig. 5.7 In these arrangements the floor structures are two-way spanning reinforced concrete slabs. This allows more freedom in the positioning of loadbearing walls than is possible with one-way spanning timber or pre-cast concrete floors.

Trussed rafters spanning between external walls

Pre-cast concrete floor slabs spanning between cross-walls

Fig. 5.8 Typical arrangement of elements in traditional loadbearing masonry structure.

Where greater freedom to plan the interior of a building is required or where large interior spaces are desirable, it is usually necessary to adopt some type of frame structure. This can allow the total elimination of structural walls,

Fig. 5.9 A typical multi-storey frame structure in which a skeleton of steel beams and columns supports a floor of reinforced concrete slabs. Walls are non-structural and can be positioned to suit space-planning requirements.

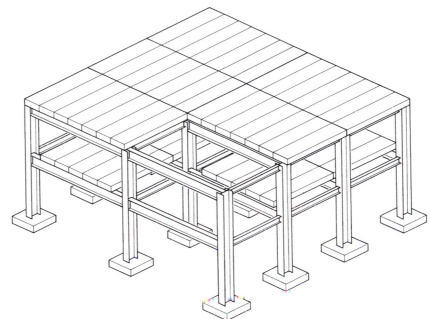

and large interior spaces can be achieved as well as significant variations in floor plans between different levels in multi-storey buildings.

The principal characteristic of the frame is that it is a skeletal structure consisting of beams supported by columns, with some form of slab floor and roof (Fig. 5.9). The walls are usually non-structural (some may be used as vertical-plane bracing) and are supported entirely by the beam-column system. The total volume which is occupied by the structure is less than with loadbearing walls, and individual elements therefore carry larger areas of floor or roof and are subjected to greater amounts of internal force. Strong materials such as steel and reinforced concrete must normally be used. Skeleton frames of timber, which is a relatively weak material, must be of short span (max 5 m) if floor loading is carried. Larger spans are possible with single-storey timber structures, especially if efficient types of element such as triangulated trusses are used, but the maximum spans are always smaller than those of equivalent steel structures.

The most basic types of frame are arranged as a series of identical 'plane-frames' of rectangular geometry[2], positioned parallel to one another to form rectangular or square column grids; the resulting buildings have forms which are predominantly rectilinear in both plan and cross-section (Fig. 5.9). A common variation of the above is obtained if triangulated elements are used for the horizontal parts of the structure (Fig. 5.10). Typical beam-column arrangements for single and multi-storey frames are shown in Figs 5.11 to 5.13; note that systems of primary and secondary beams are used for both floor and roof structures. These allow a reasonably even distribution of internal force to be achieved between the various elements within a particular floor or roof structure. In Fig. 5.12, for example, the primary beam AB supports a larger area of floor than the secondary beam CD, and therefore carries more load. The magnitudes of the internal forces in each are similar, however, because the span of AB is shorter[3].

2 A plane-frame is simply a frame with all elements in a single plane.
3 The critical internal force is bending moment, the magnitude of which depends on the span (see Section 2.3.3).

Fig. 5.10 In this steel frame, efficient triangulated elements carry the roof load. Floor loads are supported on less efficient solid-web beams with I-shaped 'improved' cross-sections.

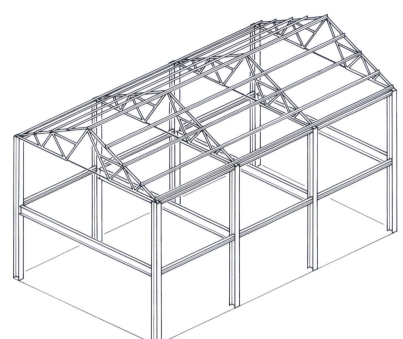

Fig. 5.11 A typical arrangement of primary and secondary beams in a single-storey steel frame. All beams have 'improved' triangulated profiles.

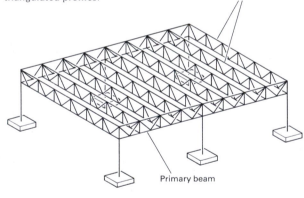

Secondary beam

Primary beam

Fig. 5.12 Typical floor layouts for multi-storey steel frames.

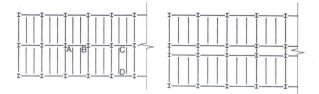

Fig. 5.13 'Improved' elements are used for all beams and columns in steel frames. In this case I-section beams are used for the floor structure and more efficient triangulated elements in the roof. The greater complexity and higher efficiency of the latter are justified by the lighter roof loading (see Section 6.2). (Photo: Pat Hunt)

Skeleton frames can be of either the discontinuous or the continuous type. Steel and timber frames are normally discontinuous and reinforced concrete frames are normally continuous. In fully discontinuous frames all the joints between beams and columns are of the hinge type (Fig. 5.14). This renders the basic form unstable and reduces its efficiency by isolating elements from each other and preventing the transfer of bending moment between them (Fig. 5.15 – see also Appendix 3). Stability is provided in the discontinuous frame by a separate bracing system, which can take a number of forms (see Figs 2.10 to 2.13). The need both to ensure stability and to provide adequate support for all areas of floor with hinge-joined elements normally requires that discontinuous frames be given regular geometries (Fig. 5.16).

If the connections in a frame are rigid, a continuous structure normally results which is both self-bracing and highly statically indeterminate (see Appendix 3). Continuous frames are therefore generally more elegant than their discontinuous equivalents; elements are lighter, spans longer and the absence of vertical-plane bracing allows more open interiors to be achieved. These advantages, together with the general planning freedom

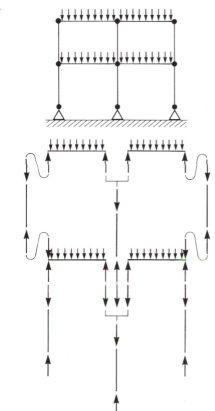

Fig. 5.15 Preliminary analysis of a discontinuous frame. Under gravitational load the horizontal elements carry pure bending and the vertical elements axial compression. Sharing or shedding of bending moment between elements is not possible through hinge joints.

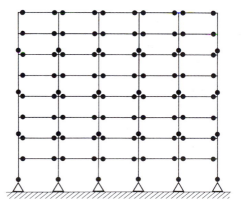

Fig. 5.14 A typical arrangement for a discontinuous multi-storey frame. All beam end connections are of the hinge type as are the column joints, which occur at alternate storey levels. The arrangement is highly unstable and requires a separate bracing system to resist horizontal load.

Fig. 5.16 Single-storey steel framework. Although some of the structural connections here are rigid, the majority of the horizontal elements have hinge joints. The regularity of the arrangement and the presence of a triangulated bracing girder in the horizontal plane (top left) are typical of a discontinuous framework. (Photo: Photo-Mayo Ltd)

Fig. 5.17 Florey Building, Oxford, UK, 1971; James Stirling, architect. The Florey Building, with its crescent-shaped plan, complex cross-section and glazed wall, illustrates how the geometric freedom made possible by a continuous frame of *in situ* concrete can be exploited. (Photo: P. Macdonald)

Fig. 5.18 Miller House, Connecticut, USA, 1970; Peter Eisenman, architect. Eisenman is one of a number of American architects, including Richard Meier (see Fig. 1.9), who have exploited the opportunities made possible by the continuous framework. This type of geometry, with its intersecting grids and contrasts of solid and void is only possible with a continuous structure.

Fig. 5.19 Willis, Faber and Dumas office, Ipswich, UK, 1974; Foster Associates, architects; Anthony Hunt Associates, structural engineers. The coffered floor slab is a flat-slab structure with an 'improved' cross-section. (Photo: Pat Hunt)

which a high degree of structural continuity allows, means that more complex geometries than are possible with discontinuous structures can be adopted (Figs 5.17, 5.18 and 1.9).

Due to the ease with which continuity can be achieved and to the absence of the 'lack-of-fit' problem (see Appendix 3), *in situ* reinforced concrete is a particularly suitable material for continuous frames. The degree of continuity which is possible even allows the beams in a frame to be eliminated and a two-way spanning slab to be supported directly on columns to form what is called a 'flat-slab' structure (Figs 5.19 and 7.33). This is both highly efficient in its use of material and fairly simple to construct. The Willis, Faber and Dumas building (Figs 1.6, 5.19 and 7.37) has a type of flat-slab structure and this building demonstrates many of the advantages of continuous structures; the geometric freedom which structural continuity allows is particularly well illustrated.

5.3 Semi-form-active structures

Semi-form-active structures have forms whose geometry is neither post-and-beam nor form-active. The elements therefore contain the full range of internal force types (i.e. axial thrust, bending moment and shear force). The magnitudes of the bending moments, which are of course the most difficult of the internal forces to resist efficiently, depend on the extent to which the shape is different from the form-active shape for the loads. The bending moments are significantly smaller, however, than those which occur in post-and-beam structures of equivalent span.

Semi-form-active structures are usually adopted as support systems for buildings for one of two reasons. They may be chosen because it is necessary to achieve greater efficiency than a post-and-beam structure would allow, because a long span is involved or because the applied load is light (see Section 6.2). Alternatively, a semi-form-active structure may be adopted because the shape of the building which is to be supported is such that neither a very simple post-and-beam structure nor a highly efficient fully form-active structure can be accommodated within it.

Figure 5.20 shows a typical example of a type of semi-form-active frame structure which is frequently adopted to achieve long spans in conjunction with light loads. It can be

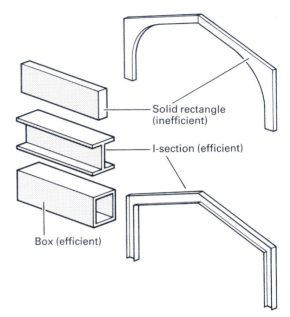

Fig. 5.20 The ubiquitous portal frame is a semi-form-active structure. The main elements in this example have 'improved' I-shaped cross-sections. (Photo: Conder)

Fig. 5.21 The efficiency of the semi-form-active portal frame is affected by the shapes of cross-section and longitudinal profile which are used. Variation of the depth of the cross-section and the use of I- or box-sections are common forms of 'improvement'. The structure type is highly versatile and is used over a wide range of spans.

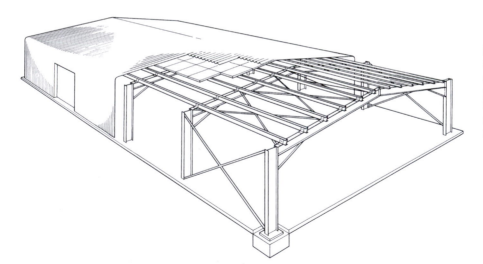

Fig. 5.22 A typical arrangement of semi-form-active portal frames forming the structure of a single-storey building.

constructed in steel, reinforced concrete or timber (Fig. 5.21). A variety of profiles and cross-sections are used for the frame elements, ranging from solid elements with rectangular cross-sections in the cases of reinforced concrete and laminated timber, to 'improved' elements in the case of steel. As with other types of frame, the range of spans which can be achieved is large. In its most common form, this type of structure consists of a series of identical plane rigid frames arranged parallel to one another to form a rectangular plan (Fig. 5.22).

5.4 Form-active structures

Fully form-active structures are normally used only in circumstances where a special structural requirement to achieve a high degree of structural efficiency exists, either because the span involved is very large or because a structure of exceptionally light weight is required. They have geometries which are more complicated than post-and-beam or semi-form-active types and they produce buildings which have distinctive shapes (Figs iii and 5.23 to 5.25).

Included in this group are compressive shells, tensile cable networks and air-supported tensile-membrane structures. In almost all cases more than one type of element is required, especially in tensile systems which must normally have compressive as well as tensile parts, and form-active shapes are frequently chosen for the compressive elements as well as for the tensile

elements (see Fig. 7.18). In the case of large building envelopes, the loads which are applied are predominantly of the distributed rather than the concentrated type and the form-active geometry is therefore curved (see Chapter 4). Although a certain amount of variety of shape is possible with this type of structure, depending on the conditions of support which are provided, the distinctive doubly-curved geometry of the form-active element is something which must be accepted by a designer who contemplates using this type of arrangement.

Form-active structures are almost invariably statically indeterminate and this, together with the fact that they are difficult to construct, makes them very expensive in the present age, despite the fact that they make an efficient use of structural material. The level of complexity which is involved in their design and construction can be appreciated by considering just a few of the special design problems which

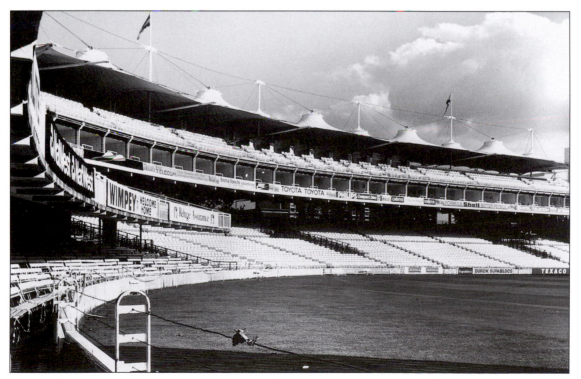

Fig. 5.23 Grandstand at Lord's Cricket Ground, London, UK, 1987; Michael Hopkins & Partners, architects; Ove Arup & Partners, structural engineers. The canopies which form the roof of this building are form-active tensile membranes.

(a)

Fig. 5.24 Barton Malow Silverdome. A very large span is achieved here with a cable-reinforced air-supported membrane, which is a tensile form-active structure.

Fig. 5.25 Brynmawr Rubber Factory, Brynmawr, UK, 1952; Architects Co-Partnership, architects; Ove Arup & Partners, structural engineers. The principal enclosing elements here are compressive form-active, elliptical paraboloid shell roofs. (Photo: *Architectural Review*)

(b)

they create. The tensile envelopes, for example, always assume the form-active shape for the load which acts on them no matter what their initial geometry may have been. This is a consequence of their complete lack of rigidity and it means that considerable care must be taken in their manufacture to ensure that the tailoring of the membrane or network is correct. If this is not done and a membrane with a non-form-active geometry is produced, initially it will nevertheless be forced into the form-active shape when the load is applied, causing folds and wrinkles to develop which are both unsightly and result in concentrations of stress. Many other technical difficulties, associated with the attachment of the membranes to their supports and with their behaviour in response to dynamic loads, also arise in connection with the design of tensile form-active structures.

In the case of the compressive version of the form-active structure, the penalty which is incurred if it is not given the true form-active shape for the load is that bending stress occurs in the membrane. If this happens unintentionally there is a risk of strength failure, and it is therefore desirable that the exact geometry of the true form-active shape should be determined during the design process and that the structure be made to conform to it. Two problems arise, however. Firstly, the geometry of the form-active shape is very complex and is difficult to determine accurately, and thus difficult to reproduce exactly in a real structure. In particular, the radius of curvature of the surface is not constant and this makes both the analysis of the structure and its construction difficult. Secondly, real structures are always subjected to a variety of different forms of loading, which means that the required form-active shape changes as loads change. This does not present an insuperable problem in the case of tensile form-active-structures because, being flexible, these can simply adjust their geometry to take up the different shapes which are required. So long as the change in load is not too extreme, the necessary adjustment can be accommodated without the risk of serious wrinkles developing. Compressive forms must be rigid, however, and so only one geometry is possible. Therefore some bending stress will inevitably arise in a compressive form-active structure due to changes which occur to the

loading. Thus these structures must be given the strength to resist bending stress and they must be made thicker than would be necessary if only direct stress was present.

The fact that bending stress can never be totally eliminated from compressive form-active structures means that they are inevitably less efficient than their tensile equivalents. It also means that the adoption of a true form-active shape, with all the complications which this involves, such as varying radii of curvature, is rarely considered to be justified. A compromise is frequently made in which a doubly-curved shape, which is close to the form-active shape but which has a much simpler geometry, is adopted. These more practical shapes achieve greater simplicity either by having a constant radius of curvature, as in a spherical dome, or by being translational forms, which can be generated by simple curves such as parabolas or ellipses. The hyperbolic paraboloid and the elliptical paraboloid (Fig. 5.25) are examples of the latter. These shapes are simpler to analyse and to construct than true form-active shapes and by adopting them the designer elects to pay the penalty of lower efficiency to achieve relative ease of design and construction.

5.5 Conclusion

In this chapter the three basic types of structural arrangement have been described and a small selection of each has been illustrated. A great number of variations is possible within each type, depending on the nature of the elements of which they are composed. An ability to place a structure within the appropriate category forms a useful basis for assessing its performance and the appropriateness of its selection for a particular application.

Chapter 6

The critical appraisal of structures

6.1 Introduction

It is said, albeit usually by critics, that creative activity is enriched by criticism. The world of structural engineering, in which a very large number of artefacts are created continuously, is, however, curiously devoid of a climate of criticism, and few engineering structures receive anything like the critical attention which is accorded to even the most modest of buildings. There is therefore no tradition of criticism in structural engineering comparable to that which exists in architecture and the other arts[1].

Design has been described as a problem-solving activity, an iterative process in which self-criticism by the designer forms an essential part. It is with this type of criticism, rather than the journalistic type alluded to above, that this chapter is principally concerned. It is not proposed, therefore, to deal comprehensively here with the subject of structural criticism but simply to identify the technical factors by which the merits of structures may be assessed.

Engineering is principally concerned with economy of means – a structure may be considered to have been well engineered if it fulfils its function with a minimum input of materials and other resources. This does not mean that the most efficient[2] structure, which produces the required load-carrying capacity with a minimum weight of material, is necessarily the best; several other technical factors, including the complexity of the construction process and the subsequent durability of the structure, will affect the judgement of whether or not a structure is satisfactory. Frequently, the technical requirements conflict with one another. For example, as was seen in Chapter 4, efficient forms are invariably complex and therefore difficult to design, construct and maintain.

This dichotomy between efficiency and simplicity of form is a fundamental aspect of structural design. The final geometry which is adopted is always a compromise between these two properties, and the elegance with which this compromise is achieved is one of the principal criteria of good structural design. In the context of architecture it affects the relationship between the appearance and the performance of a structure. The factors on which the nature of the best compromise depends are reviewed here.

6.2 Complexity and efficiency in structural design

A fundamental engineering requirement is that economy of means should be achieved. The

---

1 The controversy over whether or not structural engineering is an art will not be entered into here. This is discussed at length in Billington, D. P., *The Tower and the Bridge*, MIT Press, Cambridge, MA, 1983 and Holgate, A., *The Art in Structural Design*, Clarendon Press, Oxford, 1986. See also Addis, W. B., *The Art of the Structural Engineer*, Artemis, London, 1994.

2 As in Chapter 4, structural efficiency is considered here in terms of the weight of material which has to be provided to carry a given amount of load. The efficiency of a structure is regarded as high if the ratio of its strength to its weight is high.

overall level of resources committed to a project should be as small as possible. A sensible balance should be struck between the complexity required for high structural efficiency (see Chapter 4) and the ease of design, construction and maintenance which the adoption of a simple arrangement allows. It is the nature of this compromise which must be assessed by the critic who wishes to judge the merits of a structure.

The aspects of structure on which efficiency depends, where efficiency is judged primarily in terms of the weight of material which must be provided to give a particular load-carrying capacity, were outlined in Chapter 4. It was shown that the volume and therefore the weight of material required for a structure is dependent principally on its overall form in relation to the pattern of applied load and on the shapes of the structural elements in both cross-section and longitudinal profile. A basic classification system based on the concepts of form-active shape and 'simple' and 'improved' cross-sections and longitudinal profiles was described; this allows judgements to be made concerning the level of efficiency which is likely to be achieved with a particular structural arrangement. Form-active shapes such as tensile cables and compressive vaults were seen to be potentially the most efficient, and non-form-active beams the least efficient.

A property of structures which was demonstrated by this ordering of elements is that the higher the efficiency the more complex the form[3]. This is generally the case even when relatively minor measures are taken to improve structural efficiency, such as the use of I-shaped or box-shaped cross-sections for beams instead of solid rectangles, or a triangulated internal geometry instead of a solid web for a girder.

The complicated geometry which must be adopted to obtain high efficiency affects the ease with which a structure can be constructed and its constituent components manufactured, and its subsequent durability. For example, a triangulated framework is both more difficult to construct and more difficult to maintain subsequently than is a solid-web beam. The designer of a structure must therefore balance these considerations against the natural desire to minimise the amount of material involved. The level of efficiency which has been achieved should be appropriate for the individual circumstances of the structure.

It is not possible to specify precisely the level of efficiency which should be achieved in a particular structure, such is the complexity of the interrelationships between the various factors involved. It is possible, however, to identify two main influences on this desirable level, namely the size of the span which a structure must achieve and the intensity of the external load which it will carry. The longer the span, the greater is the need for high efficiency; the higher the level of load which is carried, the lower can the efficiency be. These two influences are in fact different aspects of the same phenomenon, namely a requirement to maintain the ratio of self-weight to external load at a more or less constant level. Implicit in this statement is the idea that, in order to achieve the ideal of maximum economy of means, the level of complexity of a structure should be the minimum consistent with achieving a reasonable level of efficiency.

The effect on efficiency of increasing span is demonstrated in the very simple example of a beam of rectangular cross-section carrying a uniformly distributed load (Fig. 6.1). In the figure, two beams of different spans are shown, each carrying the same intensity of load. The one with the longer span must have a greater depth so as to have adequate strength. The self-weight of each beam is directly proportional to its depth and so the ratio of load carried to self-weight per unit length of beam (the structural efficiency) is less favourable for the larger span.

---

3 The concept of the optimum structure provides further evidence that complexity is necessary to achieve high levels of efficiency – see Cox, H. L., *The Design of Structures of Least Weight*, Pergamon, London, 1965 and Majid, K. I., *Optimum Design of Structures*, Newnes-Butterworth, London, 1974.

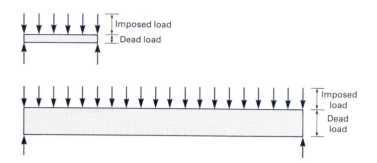

Another way of demonstrating the same effect would be to use a beam element with a particular cross-section across a range of spans. The strength of the beam – its moment of resistance (see Appendix 2.3) – would be constant. At small spans the maximum bending moment generated by the self-weight would be low and the beam might have a reasonable capacity to carry additional load. As the span was increased the bending moment generated by the self-weight would increase and an ever greater proportion of the strength available would have to be devoted to carrying the self-weight. Eventually a span would be reached in which all of the strength available was required to support only the self-weight. The structural efficiency of the beam (its capacity to carry external load divided by its weight) would steadily diminish as the span increased.

Thus, in the case of a horizontal span, which is the most common type of structure found in architecture, the efficiency of an element with a particular shape of cross-section decreases as the span increases. To maintain a constant level of efficiency over a range of spans, different shapes of cross-section have to be used. More efficient shapes have to be used as the span is increased if a constant level of load to self-weight (efficiency) is to be maintained.

The general principle involved here is that the larger the span, the greater the number of 'improvements' required to maintain a constant level of efficiency. The principle may be extended to the overall form of a structure and indeed to the full range of factors which affect efficiency. Thus, to maintain a constant level of efficiency over a wide range of span,

simple non-form-active structures might be appropriate for short spans. As the span is increased, elements with progressively more of the features associated with efficiency are required to maintain a constant level of efficiency. At intermediate spans semi-form-active types are required, again progressing through the range of possibilities for 'improvement'. For the very largest spans, form-active structures have to be specified.

The relationship between structural efficiency and intensity of applied load, which is the other significant factor affecting 'economy of means', can also be fairly easily demonstrated. Taking again the simple example of a beam with a rectangular cross-section, the weight of this increases in direct proportion with its depth while its strength increases with the square of its depth (see Appendix 2.3). Thus, if the external load is increased by a factor of two the doubling in strength which is required to carry this can be achieved by an increase in the depth which is less than twofold (in fact, by a factor of 1.4). The increase in the weight of the beam is therefore also less than twofold and the overall efficiency of the element carrying the double load is greater. Thus, for a given span and shape of cross-section, the efficiency of the element increases as the intensity of load increases and larger cross-sections must be specified. Conversely, if a particular level of efficiency is required, this can be achieved with less efficient shapes of cross-section when heavier loads are carried (the relationship between efficiency and shape of cross-section is discussed in Section 4.3 and in Appendix 2.3).

An examination of extant structures demonstrates that the majority are in fact designed in accordance with an awareness of the relationship between span, load and efficiency described above. Although it is always possible to find exceptions, it is nevertheless generally true that structures of short span are mainly produced in configurations which are inefficient, i.e. post-and-beam non-form-active arrangements with 'simple' shapes in cross-section and longitudinal profile. As spans increase the incidence of features which produce increased efficiency is greater and structures with very long spans are always constructed in efficient formats. This is very obvious in bridge engineering, as is illustrated in Fig. 6.2, and can be demonstrated to be broadly true of building structures.

The most obvious demonstration of the influence of load intensity on the type of element which is employed is found in multi-storey frameworks. The principal loads on the horizontal structural elements of these are gravitational loads and, of these, floor loads are of much higher intensity than roof loads (from two to ten times as much). In multi-storey frameworks it is very common for different structural configurations to be used for floor and roof structures, with roof structures being given more of the features which are associated with greater structural efficiency, even though the spans are the same (see Fig. 5.13).

From all of the foregoing it is possible to picture a fairly tidy taxonomy of structures in which the type of structure which would be most suitable for a particular application would range from the simplest post-and-beam non-form-active types for very short spans, through a series of 'improved' non-form-active or semi-form-active types in the medium span range, to form-active structures for the longest spans. Because the underlying requirement of structural design is to produce a ratio of load to self-weight which is approximately constant, the precise levels of span at which transitions from less to more efficient types of element would be appropriate would be affected by the

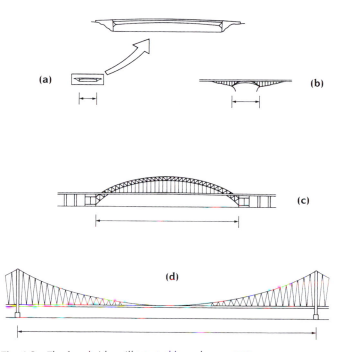

Fig. 6.2   The four bridges illustrated here demonstrate the tendency for structural complexity to increase with span due to the need for greater efficiency. (a) Luzancy Bridge; span 55 m, post-and-beam. (b) Salginatobel Bridge; span 90 m, compressive-form-active arch with solid cross-section. (c) Bayonne Bridge, span 504 m, compressive form-active arch with 'improved' triangulated longitudinal profile. (d) Severn Bridge, span 990 m, tensile form-active.

load intensity: the higher the load carried, the longer would be the span at which the change to a more efficient type would be justified. The technical factor which determines the precise level of span for which a particular structural configuration is most appropriate is the fundamental engineering requirement that economy of means should be achieved.

One indicator of the extent to which the correct balance between complexity (and therefore efficiency) and simplicity has been achieved is cost. Although monetary cost is not strictly a technical aspect of the performance of a structure it does give an indication of the level of resources of all kinds which will have been involved in its realisation. Cost is therefore a measure of the level of economy of means which has been achieved and is frequently crucial in determining the balance of efficiency and complexity which is appropriate in a particular case.

Cost is, of course, an artificial yardstick which is affected by the ways in which a society chooses to order its priorities. These are likely, increasingly, to be related to the realities of shortages of materials and energy, and to the need to reduce levels of industrial pollution. Cost, which, in the economic context of the modern world of the twentieth century, was largely unrelated to these aspects of reality and which was eschewed by critics of architecture as a measure of the worth of a building, may, in the twenty-first century become an important consideration in the assessment of the appropriateness of a structure.

As with other aspects of design the issues which affect cost are related in complicated ways. For example, in considering cost in relation to structural design, the designer must take into account not only the cost of the structure itself but also the effect of the selection of a particular structure type on other building costs. If, for example, it proved possible to reduce the cost of a multi-storey structure by slightly increasing the structural depth of each floor, this saving might be counteracted by an increase in the cost of the cladding and other building components. If a structure type were selected which, although more expensive than an alternative, allowed the building to be erected more quickly (e.g. a steel rather than a reinforced concrete frame), the increase in the cost of the structure might be more than offset by the savings involved in having the building completed more quickly. The issue of cost, in relation to structural design, must therefore involve a consideration of other issues besides those which are solely concerned with the structure. Such factors are especially important when the cost of the structure itself may form a relatively small proportion of the total cost of the building. In spite of these reservations, it is nevertheless possible to make certain general observations concerning the issue of purely structural costs.

Cost, and in particular the relationship between labour costs and material costs in the economy within which the structure is constructed, strongly influences the ratio of load carried to self-weight which is appropriate within a particular economic regime. This is a major factor in determining the spans at which the transition from less to more structurally efficient forms are made.

This can be illustrated by considering the relationship between material and labour costs for a particular structure. Consider, for example, the problem of a single-storey building of moderate span – an example might be the Renault Centre (Fig. 3.19). It may be assumed that a steel framework is a sensible form of structure to support such an enclosure but the range of structural possibilities available to the designer is very large. Simple post-and-beam forms with parallel-sided beams would be the least structurally efficient option. Semi-form-active portal frameworks with triangulated elements would be more efficient. A cable supported structure or tent would give the greatest efficiency in the use of material. The higher the efficiency, the greater the complexity and therefore the higher would be the design and construction costs.

The relationship between material and labour costs of all kinds is represented diagramatically in Fig. 6.3. The optimum level of efficiency corresponds with the minimum point in the curve indicating the total costs; this will correspond to a particular type of structure. Figure 6.3 also illustrates the effect of a variation in labour cost. The effect of an increase in labour costs, relative to material costs, is to reduce the level of efficiency at which the optimum level of economy of means occurs. This effect accounts for variations in patterns of building in different parts of the world. The higher the cost of materials in relation to labour, the greater is the incentive to achieve high efficiency and the smaller is the span at which the transition from less to more efficient and therefore more complex configurations is justified.

Extreme examples of this are found in tribal societies in which the economic conditions are such that very complex structural forms are used for structures of relatively short span. The

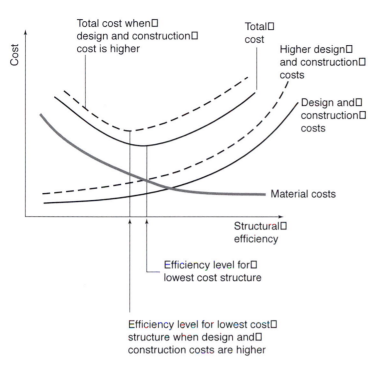

Total cost when
design and construction
cost is higher

Total
cost

Higher design
and construction
costs

Design and
construction
costs

Cost

Material costs

Structural
efficiency

Efficiency level for
lowest cost structure

Efficiency level for lowest cost
structure when design and
construction costs are higher

Fig. 6.3 The relationship between structural efficiency and structural costs for a structure with a particular span and load condition are shown here diagrammatically. The quantity and therefore cost of material decreases as more efficient types of structure are used. The latter have more complex forms, however, so the cost of construction and design increases with increased structural efficiency. The curve showing total cost has a minimum point which gives the level of efficiency which is most cost-effective for that particular structure. If labour costs increase in relation to material costs, the location of the minimum in the total cost curve is displaced to the left indicating that a structural form of lower efficiency will now be the most cost-effective.

Bedouin tent, the igloo (Fig. 1.2) and the yurt (Fig. 6.4), all of which are form-active structures, may represent the very many examples which might be cited. The availability of ample reserves of labour to build and maintain complex structures and the fact that they are the most effective ways of using locally available materials are responsible for this use of a wide range of different forms for short spans, all of them very efficient.

The situation in the industrialised societies of the developed world is that labour is expensive in relation to material. This favours the use of forms which are structurally inefficient but which are straightforward to build. The majority of the structures found in the developed world are inefficient post-and-beam types, an excellent example of the profligacy with material of the industrialised culture.

It is possible to suggest that for a particular span and load requirement and within a particular set of economic circumstances there will be a limited number of appropriate structure

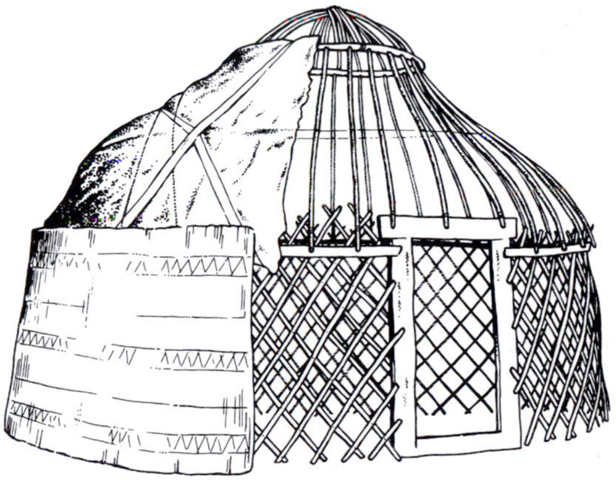

Fig. 6.4 The yurt is the traditional house of the nomadic peoples of Asia. It consists of a highly sophisticated arrangement of self-bracing semi-form-active timber structural elements which support a non-structural felt skin. It is light and its domed shape, which combines maximum internal volume with minimum surface area, is ideal for heat conservation and also minimises wind resistance. When judged by purely technical criteria this building-type will stand comparison with many of those produced by the so-called technological societies of the late twentieth century.

types. These will range from the simplest post-and-beam non-form-active types for the shortest spans, to form-active shells and cable structures for the largest spans. The majority of buildings conform to this pattern but there are exceptions. Some of these could be regarded as simply ill-considered designs. Others can be justified by special circumstances.

For example, if there is a significant requirement for a lightweight structure, this would justify the use of a more efficient structural form than might otherwise be considered appropriate for the span. Perhaps the most extreme example of this is the backpacker's tent, an extremely short-span building for which a tensile form-active structure (the most sophisticated and most efficient type of structure) is used. The requirement for minimum weight is, of course, the justification in this case. Other examples are buildings which are temporary or which must be transported, such as those which are designed to house travelling exhibitions (see Fig. 7.24) or travelling theatres.

Another reason for adopting a structure type which might otherwise be considered

inappropriate for the span or load involved might be that the building had to be built quickly. Where speed of erection is given the highest priority, a lightweight steel framework might be a sensible choice even though other considerations such as the shortness of the span might not justify this. The use of lightweight steel framing for short-span buildings such as houses, of which the Hopkins House (Fig. 6.5) is a special case, is an example of this.

Sometimes, where the structure is part of the aesthetic programme of the building, a structure type is selected for its visual features rather than from a consideration of purely technical issues. Many of the structures which are found in so-called 'high-tech' architecture fall into this category. It is always possible to find examples of buildings in which a client was prepared to pay excessively and therefore commit excessive resources in terms of either materials or labour, in order to have a spectacular structure which would be unjustified on purely technical grounds.

A technical issue which has not so far been considered, but which should form part of any

Fig. 6.5 Hopkins House, London, UK, 1977; Michael Hopkins, architect; Anthony Hunt Associates, structural engineers. The very short spans involved here would not normally justify the use of complex triangulated elements for the horizontal structure. Ease and speed of erection were the main technical reasons for their selection. The visual excitement which they produce was, nevertheless, the principal reason for their adoption. (Photo: Anthony Hunt Associates)

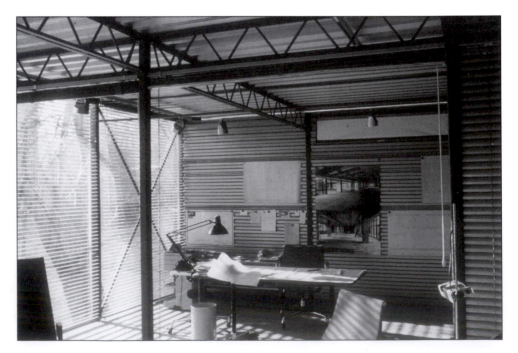

thorough assessment of a structure, is its durability. Both the durability properties of the individual constituent materials and the durability implications of combinations of materials must be considered. In some cases, where a structure will be subjected to a particularly hostile environment, the question of durability will be given a high priority at the design stage and will affect both the choice of material and the choice of form. More often, choices will be dictated by other criteria – such as span and load – and the question then to be answered is whether the material has been used sensibly. If, for example, the material selected is steel, which, in its unprotected state is one of the least corrosion-resistant materials, the problem of durability should be recognised. This would mitigate against using steel exposed on the exterior of a building, especially in humid climates.

The structure should be capable of fulfilling the function for which it is designed throughout the intended life of the building, without requiring that an unreasonable amount of maintenance be carried out on it. This raises the question of what is reasonable in this context, which brings us back to the question of economy of means and relative costs. So far as durability is concerned, a balance must be struck between initial cost and subsequent maintenance and repair costs. No definite best solution to this can be specified, but an assessment of the implications for durability must form part of any serious assessment of the merits of a structure.

6.3 Reading a building as a structural object

The idea that structural criticism should be an aspect of the standard critical appraisal of a work of architecture requires an ability, on the part of the critic, to read a building as a structural object. The classification system proposed in Chapter 4 provides a basis for this. The system is based on a categorisation of elements according to structural efficiency.

As has been discussed in Section 6.2, the measure of a good structure is not that the *highest* level of structural efficiency has been achieved, but that an *appropriate* level has been achieved. The judgement of the latter can only be made from a position of knowledge concerning the factors which affect efficiency. A few examples are now considered to demonstrate the use of the system for the appraisal of structures.

The Forth Railway Bridge[4] (Fig. 6.6) is a spectacular example of a work of more or less 'pure' engineering which makes an appropriate beginning. Although the general arrangement of the bridge may seem very complex, it may be seen to be fairly straightforward if visualised in accordance with the concepts of 'form-action' and 'improvement'. The principal elements of this structure are paired, balanced cantilevers. This configuration was adopted so that the bridge could be constructed without the use of temporary supports. The structure was self-supporting throughout the entire construction process. The cantilevers are linked by short suspended spans, a clever arrangement which allows the advantages of structural continuity to be achieved in a discontinuous structure[5].

The arrangement was therefore non-form-active and potentially inefficient. Given the spans involved, extensive measures were justified to achieve an acceptable level of efficiency. These took several forms: the profile of the main structure was made to conform to the bending-moment diagram resulting from the principal load condition (a uniformly distributed gravitational load across the whole structure) and the internal geometry of this profile was fully triangulated. The rail tracks were carried on an internal viaduct – itself a

---

4 See Macdonald, Angus J. and Boyd Whyte, I., *The Forth Bridge*, Axel Menges, Stuttgart, 1997 for a more complete description of the structure and discussion of its cultural significance.
5 See Section 5.1 and Appendix 3 for an explanation of the terms continuous and discontinuous structures.

Fig. 6.6 Basic structural arrangement of the Forth Railway Bridge, Firth of Forth, UK. This structure is a post-and-beam framework but, as with the Renault Headquarters (Figs 3.19 & 6.8), it has been 'improved' at various levels. There is more justification for the complexity in this case due to the large span involved. (Photo: A. & P. Macdonald)

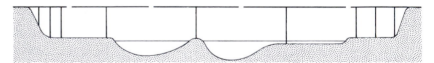

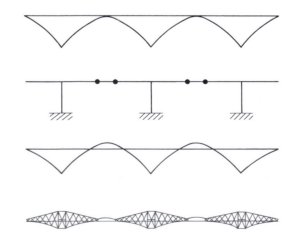

non-form-active structure 'improved' by triangulation – which was connected to the main structure only at the nodes of the triangles. Thus, the principal sub-elements of the structure carried either direct tension or direct compression. The individual sub-elements were given 'improved' cross-sections. The main compression sub-elements, for example, are hollow tubes, most of them with a cross-section which is circular, which is the most efficient shape for resisting axial compression. Thus, the structure of the Forth Railway Bridge has a basic form which is potentially rather inefficient but which was 'improved' in a number of ways.

The most common structural arrangement in the world of architecture is the post-and-beam form in which horizontal elements are supported on vertical columns or walls. In the most basic version of this, the horizontal elements are non-form-active, under the action of gravitational load, and the vertical elements are axially loaded and may therefore be regarded as form-active. Countless versions of this arrangement have been used through the centuries, and it is significant that the greatest variations are to be seen in the non-form-active horizontal elements where the advantages to be gained from the 'improvement' of cross-sections and longitudinal profiles are greatest.

The temples of Greek antiquity, of which the Parthenon in Athens (see Fig. 7.1) is the supreme example, are a very basic version of the post-and-beam arrangement. The level of efficiency achieved here is low, and this is due partly to the presence of non-form-active elements and partly to the methods used to determine the sizes and proportions of the elements. The priorities of the designers were not those of the present-day engineer, and the idea of achieving efficiency in a materialistic sense was probably the last consideration in the minds of Ictinus and his collaborators when the dimensions of the Parthenon were determined. The building is perhaps the best illustration of the fact that the achievement of structural efficiency is not a necessary requirement for great architecture.

In the twentieth century, by contrast, efficiency in the use of material was given a high priority partly in a genuine attempt to economise on material in order to save cost, but also as a consequence of the prevalence of the belief in the modernist ideal of 'rational' design. The overall geometry of the inefficient non-form-active post-and-beam form is so convenient, however, that it has nevertheless continued to be the most widely used type of architectural structure. It was normal in the modern period, however, for at least the horizontal elements to have some form of 'improvement' built into them. This was especially true of steel frameworks in which the beams and columns invariably had 'improved' I-shaped cross-sections and much use was made of the technique of internal triangulation.

In the Centre Pompidou, in Paris (Figs 6.7 and 1.10), the basic arrangement of the

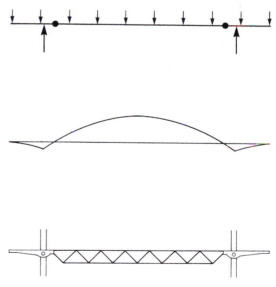

Fig. 6.7 Load, bending moment and structural diagrams for one of the principal elements in the floor structure of the Centre Pompidou, Paris, France. This is a non-form-active beam but the relatively long span involved justified the incorporation of 'improvements'. Height restrictions prevented the matching of the longitudinal profile to the bending moment diagram, except in the cantilevered 'gerberette brackets' at the extremities of the structure. Triangulation was the only form of 'improvement' which was feasible here for the main element (see also Figs 1.10, 3.17, 7.7 and 7.8).

structure is such that all of the horizontal elements are straight, non-form-active beams and this configuration is therefore potentially very inefficient. The triangulation of the main girders and the use of 'improved' shapes in cross-section and longitudinal profile of the cantilevered gerberettes (see Fig. 3.17) compensates for the potential inefficiency of the form, however, and the overall level of efficiency which was achieved may be judged to be moderate.

The framework of the Renault Building at Swindon, UK (see Fig. 3.19), may also be regarded as a post-and-beam frame as the basic form of the structure is rectilinear (Fig. 6.8). The beam-to-column junctions are rigid, however, and provide a degree of structural continuity, so that both horizontal and vertical elements are subjected to a combination of axial and bending-type internal force under the action of gravitational loads. The latter are therefore semi-form-active. Because the basic shape of the structure is markedly different from the form-active shape[6], the magnitudes of the bending moments are high and the structure is therefore potentially rather inefficient. The longitudinal profiles of the horizontal elements have, however, been 'improved' in a number of ways. The overall depth is varied in accordance with the bending-moment diagram and the profile itself is subdivided into a combination of a bar element and an I-section element, the relative positions of which are adjusted so that the bar element forms the tensile component in the combined cross-section and the I-section the compressive element[7]. The circular cross-section of the bar is a sensible shape to carry the tensile load, while the I-section of the compressive part is a suitable choice in view of the need to resist

compressive instability, which is a bending phenomenon. The cutting of circular holes from its web (see Fig. 3.19) is another form of 'improvement'. A similar breakdown of the cross-section occurs in the vertical elements, but in these the compressive components are circular hollow sections instead of I-sections. This is again sensible because these components are subjected to a greater amount of compression than their counterparts in the horizontal elements, and the circle is an ideal shape of cross-section with which to resist compression. The choice of basic form, that of a semi-form-active rectilinear framework, is potentially only moderately efficient but, as in the case of the Centre Pompidou, a number of measures have been adopted to compensate

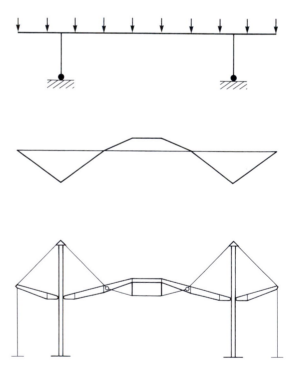

Fig. 6.8 Load, bending moment and structural diagrams of the Renault Headquarters building, Swindon, UK. The basic form of this structure is a post-and-beam non-form-active frame. 'Improvements' have been introduced at several levels: the overall profile of the structure has been made to conform to the bending moment diagram for gravitational load, the structure has been triangulated internally and some of the sub-elements have been further 'improved' by having I-shaped cross-sections and circular holes cut in their webs (see also Figs 3.19).

---

6 The load pattern on the primary structure is a series of closely-spaced concentrated loads. The form-active shape for this is similar to a catenary.

7 The bar element is sometimes above the I-section and sometimes below, depending upon the sense of the bending moment and therefore upon whether the top or the bottom of the combined section is in tension.

for this. The question of whether an appropriate overall level of efficiency has been achieved in this case is discussed in Section 7.2.2.

'Improvements' to element cross-sections are seen less often in buildings with reinforced concrete structures because concrete is both lighter and cheaper than steel, so there is not the same incentive to achieve even the moderate levels of structural efficiency of steel frameworks. Coffered slabs are used in the Willis, Faber and Dumas building (see Figs 1.6 and 5.19), however, and are examples of 'improved' non-form-active elements in a post-and-beam, reinforced concrete arrangement. Versions of this type of 'improvement' are incorporated into most reinforced concrete structures if the span is greater than 6 m.

These few examples of structural classification serve to illustrate the usefulness of the system described in Section 4.4 as a means of assessing the level of efficiency achieved in a structure. It should never be assumed, however, when judging the appropriateness of a structural design for a particular application, that the most efficient structure is necessarily the best. Even in the case of a 'purely' engineering structure, such as a bridge, other factors such as the level of complexity of the construction process or the implications of the form for long-term durability have to be considered and there are many situations in which a simple beam with a rectangular cross-section – perhaps the least efficient of structural forms – constitutes the best technical solution to a structural support problem. The question to be decided when a technical judgement is made about a structure is not so much one of whether the maximum possible level of efficiency has been achieved as of whether an *appropriate* level has been achieved.

6.4 Conclusion

Any formulation of the criteria by which the merits of a structure could be judged is inevitably controversial. Most people would, however, feel able to agree with the statement that the principal objective of engineering design is to provide an object which will function satisfactorily with maximum economy of means. This is summed up in the old engineering adage that 'an engineer is someone who can do for £1 what any fool can do for £3'.

The assessment of whether or not a reasonable level of economy of means has been achieved involves the examination of a number of different aspects of the design of an artefact. It is principally a matter of being satisfied that a reasonable balance has been achieved between the quantity of material used, the complexity of the design and construction processes, and the subsequent durability and dependability of the artefact. In the context of structural engineering, the achievement of economy of means is not simply a matter of minimising the amount of material which is required for a structure, but rather of making the best possible use of all the material, effort and energy which are involved in its production. Because these factors are interrelated in complicated ways, the overall judgement required is not straightforward.

One measure of the extent to which economy of means has been achieved is cost, since the cost of the structure in monetary terms is related to the total input of resources to the structure. Cost is, of course, almost entirely an artificial yardstick dependent on the current market prices of labour, energy and materials. It is always related to a particular economic culture, but also to the resources, both human and environmental, which a society has at its disposal. All of these considerations are subject to change over time.

It is possible to argue that from a purely engineering point of view the structure which is cheapest constitutes the best solution to the problem of supporting an enclosure. In most cultures the majority of 'ordinary' buildings are in fact constructed in such a way as to minimise cost. The judgement of whether or not a particular structure constitutes good engineering could therefore be made by comparing it to the mainstream of contemporary practice. If it is broadly similar to the majority of comparable structures it is probably well engineered.

By this criterion the standard and ubiquitous portal-frame shed, which is used to house supermarkets and warehouses throughout the industrialised world, would qualify as good engineering and the so-called 'high-tech' supersheds which appeared in the architectural journals in the 1980s would not, and would at best be regarded as expensive toys. It is necessary to bear in mind that what is being discussed here is engineering and not architecture although, in the context of the need to evolve forms of building which meet the requirements of sustainability, these disciplines may have to become more closely related in the future. If there were more contact between these two extremes of building strategy, this might benefit both the visual and the engineering environments.

It must always be borne in mind that engineering is not about image making. It is about the provision of artefacts which are useful. If the problem to be solved is very difficult technically – e.g. a very long span building, a vehicle which must move with great speed or fly through the air, or a structure which supports life in an inhospitable environment – then the object which is created is likely to be spectacular in some way and, if a building structure, may be visually exciting. If the problem is not technically difficult – e.g. a building of modest span – then the best engineering solution will also be modest although it may nevertheless be subtle; if it is well designed and elegant from an engineering point of view it will be exciting to those who appreciate engineering design. Twentieth-century modernists who believed that the 'celebration' of the 'excitement' of technology was a necessary part of all architectural expression applied different criteria to the assessment of structure.

Chapter 7

Structure and architecture

7.1 Introduction

Two related but distinct issues are discussed in this chapter. These are the relationship between structure and architecture and the relationship between structural engineers and architects. Each of these may take more than one form, and the type which is in play at any time influences the effect which structure has on architecture. These are issues which shed an interesting sidelight on the history of architecture.

Structure and architecture may be related in a wide variety of ways ranging between the extremes of complete domination of the architecture by the structure to total disregard of structural requirements in the determination of both the form of a building and of its aesthetic treatment. This infinite number of possibilities is discussed here under six broad headings:

- *ornamentation of structure*
- *structure as ornament*
- *structure as architecture*
- *structure as form generator*
- *structure accepted*
- *structure ignored*.

As in the case of the relationship between structure and architecture, the relationship between architects and structural engineers may take a number of forms. This may range from, at one extreme, a situation in which the form of a building is determined solely by the architect with the engineer being concerned only with making it stand up, to, at the other extreme, the engineer acting as architect and determining the form of the building and all

other architectural aspects of the design. Midway between these extremes is the situation in which architect and engineer collaborate fully over the form of a building and evolve the design jointly. As will be seen, the type of relationship which is adopted has a significant effect on the nature of the resulting architecture.

7.2 The types of relationship between structure and architecture

7.2.1 Ornamentation of structure

There have been a number of periods in the history of Western architecture in which the formal logic of a favoured structural system has been allowed to influence, if not totally determine, the overall form of the buildings into which the age has poured its architectural creativity. In the periods in which this mood has prevailed, the forms that have been adopted have been logical consequences of the structural armatures of buildings. The category *ornamentation of structure*, in which the building consists of little more than a visible structural armature adjusted in fairly minor ways for visual reasons, has been one version of this.

Perhaps the most celebrated building in the Western architectural tradition in which structure dictated form was the Parthenon in Athens (Fig. 7.1). The architecture of the Parthenon is tectonic: structural requirements dictated the form and, although the purpose of the building was not to celebrate structural technology, its formal logic was celebrated as part of the visual expression. The Doric Order, which reached its greatest degree of

Fig. 7.1 The Parthenon, Athens, 5th century BC. Structure and architecture perfectly united.

refinement in this building, was a system of ornamentation evolved from the post-and-beam structural arrangement.

There was, of course, much more to the architecture of the Greek temple than ornamentation of a constructional system. The archetypal form of the buildings and the vocabulary and grammar of the ornamentation have had a host of symbolic meanings attributed to them by later commentators[1]. No attempt was made, however, by the builders of the Greek temples, either to disguise the structure or to adopt forms other than those which could be fashioned in a logical and straightforward manner from the available materials. In these buildings the structure and

the architectural expression co-exist in perfect harmony.

The same may be said of the major buildings of the mediaeval Gothic period (see Fig. 3.1), which are also examples of the relationship between structure and architecture that may be described as *ornamentation of structure*. Like the Greek temples the largest of the Gothic buildings were constructed almost entirely in masonry, but unlike the Greek temples they had spacious interiors which involved large horizontal roof spans. These could only be achieved in masonry by the use of compressive form-active vaults. The interiors were also lofty, which meant that the vaulted ceilings imposed horizontal thrust on the tops of high flanking walls and subjected them to bending moment as well as to axial internal force. The walls of these Gothic structures were therefore semi-form-active elements (see Section 4.2) carrying a combination of compressive-axial

1 For example, Scully, V., *The Earth, the Temple and the Gods*, Yale University Press, New Haven, 1979.

and bending-type internal force. The archetypical Gothic arrangement of buttresses, flying buttresses and finials is a spectacular example of a semi-form-active structure with 'improved' cross-section and profile. Virtually everything which is visible is structural and entirely justified on technical grounds. All elements were adjusted so as to be visually satisfactory: the 'cabling' of columns, the provision of capitals on columns and of string courses in walls and several other types of ornament were not essential structurally.

The strategy of *ornamentation of structure*, which was so successfully used in Greek antiquity and in the Gothic period, virtually disappeared from Western architecture at the time of the Italian Renaissance. There were several causes of this (see Section 7.3), one of which was that the structural armatures of buildings were increasingly concealed behind forms of ornamentation which were not directly related to structural function. For example, the pilasters and half columns of Palladio's Palazzo Valmarana (Fig. 7.2) and many other buildings of the period were not positioned at locations which were particularly significant structurally. They formed part of a loadbearing wall in which all parts contributed equally to the load carrying function. Such disconnection of ornament from structural function led to the structural and aesthetic agendas drifting apart and had a profound effect on the type of relationship which developed between architects and those who were responsible for the technical aspects of the design of buildings (see Section 7.3).

It was not until the twentieth century, when architects once again became interested in tectonics (i.e. the making of architecture out of those fundamental parts of a building responsible for holding it up) and in the aesthetic possibilities of the new structural technologies of steel and reinforced concrete, that the ornamental use of exposed structure re-appeared in the architectural mainstream of Western architecture. It made its tentative first appearance in the works of early Modernists such as Auguste Perret and Peter Behrens (Fig. 7.3) and was also seen in the architecture of

Fig. 7.2 The Palazzo Valmarana, Vicenza, by Andrea Palladio. The pilasters on this façade have their origins in a structural function but here form the outer skin of a structural wall. The architectural interest of the building does not lie in its structural make-up, however.

Ludwig Mies van der Rohe. The structure of the Farnsworth House, for example, is exposed and forms a significant visual element. It was also adjusted slightly for visual reasons and in that sense is an example of *ornamentation of structure*. Other more recent examples of such visual adjustments occurred in British High Tech. The exposed-steel structure of the

Fig. 7.3 AEG Turbine Hall, Berlin, 1908; Peter Behrens, architect. Glass and structure alternate on the side walls of this building and the rhythm of the steel structure forms a significant component of the visual vocabulary. Unlike in many later buildings of the Modern Movement the structure was used 'honestly'; it was not modified significantly for purely visual effect. With the exception of the hinges at the bases of the columns it was also protected within the external weathertight skin of the building. (Photo: A. Macdonald)

Reliance Controls building at Swindon, UK (Fig. 7.4), for example, by Team 4 and Tony Hunt, is a fairly straightforward technical response to the problems posed by the programmatic requirements of the building and stands up well to technical criticism[2]. It is nevertheless an example of ornamentation of structure rather than a work of pure engineering because it was adjusted in minor ways to improve its appearance. The H-section Universal Column[3] which was selected for its very slender purlins, for example, was less efficient as a bending element than the I-section Universal Beam would have been. It was used because it was considered that the tapered flanges of the Universal Beam were less satisfactory visually than the parallel-sided flanges of the Universal Column in this strictly rectilinear building.

The train shed of the International Rail Terminal at Waterloo station in London (Fig. 7.17) is another example. The overall configuration of the steel structure, which forms the principal architectural element of this building, was determined from technical considerations. The visual aspects of the design were carefully controlled, however, and the design evolved through very close collaboration between the teams of architects and engineers from the offices of Nicholas

---

2 See Macdonald, Angus J., *Anthony Hunt*, Thomas Telford, London, 2000.

3 The Universal Column and Universal Beam are the names of standard ranges of cross-sections for hot-rolled steel elements which are produced by the British steel industry.

Fig. 7.4   Reliance Controls building, Swindon, UK, 1966; Team 4, architects; Tony Hunt, structural engineer. The exposed structure of the Reliance Controls building formed an important part of the visual vocabulary. It was modified in minor ways to improve its appearance. (Photo: Anthony Hunt Associates)

Grimshaw and Partners and Anthony Hunt Associates so that it performed well aesthetically as well as technically.

These few examples serve to illustrate that throughout the entire span of the history of Western architecture from the temples of Greek antiquity to late-twentieth-century structures such as the Waterloo Terminal, buildings have been created in which architecture has been made from exposed structure. The architects of such buildings have paid due regard to the requirements of the structural technology and have reflected this in the basic forms of the buildings. The architecture has therefore been affected in a quite fundamental way by the structural technology involved. At the same time the architects have not allowed technological considerations to inhibit their architectural imagination. The results have

been well-resolved buildings which perform well when judged by either technical or non-technical criteria.

7.2.2 Structure as ornament

'The *engineer's aesthetic*[4] and architecture – two things that march together and follow one from the other.'[5]

The relationship between structure and architecture categorised here as *structure as ornament* involves the manipulation of structural elements by criteria which are

---

4   Author's italics.
5   Le Corbusier, *Towards a New Architecture*, Architectural Press, London, 1927.

principally visual and it is a relationship which has been largely a twentieth-century phenomenon. As in the category *ornamentation of structure* the structure is given visual prominence but unlike in *ornamentation of structure*, the design process is driven by visual rather than by technical considerations. As a consequence the performance of these structures is often less than ideal when judged by technical criteria. This is the feature which distinguishes *structure as ornament* from *ornamentation of structure*.

Three versions of *structure as ornament* may be distinguished. In the first of these, structure is used *symbolically*. In this scenario the devices which are associated with structural efficiency (see Chapter 4), which are mostly borrowed from the aerospace industry and from science fiction, are used as a visual vocabulary which is intended to convey the idea of progress and of a future dominated by technology. The images associated with advanced technology are manipulated freely to produce an architecture which celebrates technology. Often, the context is inappropriate and the resulting structures perform badly in a technical sense.

In the second version, spectacular exposed structure may be devised in response to *artificially created circumstances*. In this type of building, the forms of the exposed structure are justified technically, but only as the solutions to unnecessary technical problems that have been created by the designers of the building.

A third category of *structure as ornament* involves the adoption of an approach in which structure is expressed so as to produce a readable building in which technology is celebrated, but in which a *visual agenda is pursued which is incompatible with structural logic*. The lack of the overt use of images associated with advanced technology distinguishes this from the first category.

Where structure is used symbolically, a visual vocabulary which has its origins in the design of lightweight structural elements – for example the I-shaped cross-section, the triangulated girder, the circular hole cut in the web, etc. (see Chapter 4) – is used architecturally to symbolise technical excellence and to celebrate state-of-the-art technology. Much, though by no means all, of the architecture of British High Tech falls into this category. The entrance canopy of the Lloyds headquarters building in London is an example (Fig. 7.5). The curved steel elements which form the structure of this canopy, with their circular 'lightening' holes (holes cut out to lighten the element – see Section 4.3) are reminiscent of the principal fuselage elements in aircraft structures (Fig. 4.14). The complexity of the arrangement is fully justified in the aeronautical context where saving of weight is critical. The use of lightweight structures in the canopy at Lloyds merely increases the probability that it will be blown away by the wind. Its use here is entirely symbolic.

The Renault Headquarters building in Swindon, UK, by Foster Associates and Ove Arup and Partners is another example of this approach (see Figs 3.19 and 6.8). The structure of this building is spectacular and a key component of the building's image, which is intended to convey the idea of a company with a serious commitment to 'quality design'[6] and an established position at the cutting edge of technology. The building is undoubtedly elegant and it received much critical acclaim when it was completed; these design objectives were therefore achieved. Bernard Hanon, President-Directeur General, Régie Nationale des Usines Renault, on his first visit felt moved to declare: 'It's a cathedral.'[7].

The structure of the Renault building does not, however, stand up well to technical criticism. It consists of a steel-frame supporting a non-structural envelope. The basic form of the structure is of multi-bay portal frames running in two principal directions. These have many of the features associated with structural efficiency: the

6 Lambot, I. (Ed.), *Norman Foster: Foster Associates: Buildings and Projects*, Vol. 2, Watermark, Hong Kong, 1989.
7 *Ibid*.

longitudinal profile of each frame is matched to the bending-moment diagram for the principal load; the structure is trussed (i.e. separate compression and tensile elements are provided); the compressive elements, which must have some resistance to bending, have further improvements in the form of I-shaped cross-sections and circular holes cut into the webs. Although these features improve the efficiency of the structure, most of them are not justified given the relatively short spans involved (see Chapter 6). The structure is unnecessarily complicated and there is no doubt that a conventional portal-frame arrangement (a primary/secondary structural system with the portals serving as the primary structure, as in the earlier building by Foster Associates at Thamesmead, London (see Fig. 1.5)), would have provided a more economical structure for this building. Such a solution was rejected at the outset of the project by the client on the grounds that it would not have provided an appropriate image for the company[8]. The decision to use the more expensive, more spectacular structure was therefore taken on stylistic grounds.

The structure possesses a number of other features which may be criticised from a technical point of view. One of these is the placing of a significant part of it outside the weathertight envelope, which has serious implications for durability and maintenance. The configuration of the main structural elements is also far from ideal. The truss arrangement cannot tolerate reversal of load because this would place the very slender tension elements into compression. As designed, the structure is capable of resisting only downward-acting gravitational loads and not uplift. Reversal of load may tend to occur in flat-roofed buildings, however, due to the high suction forces which wind can generate. Thickening of the tensile elements to give them the capability to resist compression was considered by the architect to be unacceptable visually[9] and so this problem was solved by

Fig. 7.5 Entrance canopy, Lloyds headquarters building, London, UK, 1986; Richard Rogers and Partners, architects; Ove Arup & Partners, structural engineers. The curved steel ribs with circular 'lightening' holes are reminiscent of structures found in the aerospace industry. (Photo: Colin McWilliam)

specifying heavier roof cladding than originally intended (or indeed required) so that no reversal of load would occur. Thus the whole structure was subjected, on a permanent basis, to a larger gravitational load than was strictly necessary. A further observation which might be made regarding the structure of this building is that the imagery employed is not particularly 'cutting edge', much of it having been evolved in the

---

8 *Ibid.*
9 See Lambot, *ibid.*

earliest days of iron and steel frame design in the nineteenth century.

The sources of the visual vocabulary of structural technology used in the symbolic version of *structure as ornament* are various and, for the most part, not architectural. In some cases the source has been science fiction. More usually, images were employed which were perceived to represent very advanced technology, the most fruitful source for the latter being aeronautical engineering where the saving of weight is of paramount importance, and particularly the element with complex 'improved' cross-section and circular 'lightening' holes. Forms and element types which are associated with high structural efficiency – see Chapter 4 – are therefore employed.

One of the problems facing the designers of aircraft or vehicle structures is that the overall form is dictated by non-structural considerations. The adoption of structurally efficient form-active shapes is not possible and high efficiency has to be achieved by employing the techniques of 'improvement'. The whole vocabulary of techniques of 'improvement' – stressed-skin monocoque and semi-monocoque 'improved' beams, internal triangulation, sub-elements with I-shaped cross-sections, tapered profiles and circular 'lightening' holes – is exploited in these fields to achieve acceptable levels of efficiency (see Figs 4.13 to 4.15). It is principally this vocabulary which has been adopted by architects seeking to make a symbolic use of structure and which has often been applied in situations where the span or loading would not justify the use of complicated structures of this type on technical grounds alone.

The dichotomy between the appearance and the reality of technical excellence is nowhere more apparent than in the works of the architects of the 'Future Systems' group (Fig. 7.6):

'Future Systems believes that borrowing technology developed from structures designed to travel across land (automotive), or through water (marine), air (aviation) or vacuum (space) can help to give energy to the spirit of architecture

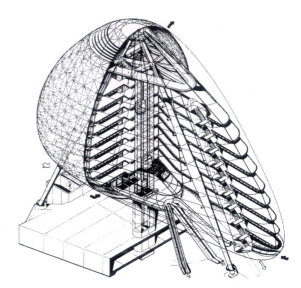

Fig. 7.6 Green Building (project), 1990: Future Systems, architects. Technology transfer or technical image-making? Many technical criticisms could be made of this design. The elevation of the building above ground level is perhaps the most obvious as this requires that an elaborate structural system be adopted including floor structures of steel-plate box-girders similar to those which are used in long-span bridge construction. There is no technical justification for their use here where a more environmentally friendly structural system, such as reinforced concrete slabs supported on a conventional column grid, would have been a more convincing choice. This would not have been so exciting visually, but it would have been more convincing in the context of the idea of a sustainable architecture.

by introducing a new generation of buildings which are efficient, elegant, versatile and exciting. This approach to shaping the future of architecture is based on the celebration of technology, not the concealment of it.'[10]

10 Jan Kaplicky and David Nixon of Future Systems quoted in the final chapter of Wilkinson, C., *Supersheds*, Butterworth Architecture, Oxford, 1991. Later in the same statement Kaplicky and Nixon declare, of the technology of vehicle and aerospace engineering, 'It is technology which is capable of yielding an architecture of sleek surfaces and slender forms – an architecture of efficiency and elegance, and even excitement.' It is clear from this quotation that it is the appearance rather than the technical reality which is attractive to Kaplicky and Nixon.

The quotation reveals a degree of naivety concerning the nature of technology. It contains the assumption that dissimilar technologies have basic similarities which produce similar solutions to quite different types of problem.

The 'borrowing of technology' referred to in the quotation above from Future Systems is problematic. Another name for this is 'technology transfer', a phenomenon in which advanced technology which has been developed in one field is adapted and modified for another. Technology transfer is a concept which is of very limited validity because components and systems which are developed for advanced technical applications, such as occur in the aerospace industry, are designed to meet very specific combinations of requirements. Unless very similar combinations occur in the field to which the technology is transferred it is unlikely that the results will be satisfactory from a technological point of view. Such transfer is therefore also misleading symbolically on any level but the most simplistic.

The claims which are made for technology transfer are largely spurious if judged by technical criteria concerned with function and efficiency. The reality of technology transfer to architecture is normally that it is the image and appearance which is the attractive element rather than the technology as such.

It is frequently stated by the protagonists of this kind of architecture[11] that, because it appears to be advanced technically, it will provide the solutions to the architectural problems posed by the worsening global environmental situation. This is perhaps their most fallacious claim. The environmental problems caused by shortages of materials and energy and by increasing levels of pollution are real technical problems which require genuine technical solutions. Both the practice and the ideology of the symbolic use of structure are fundamentally incompatible with the requirements of a sustainable architecture. The methodology of the symbolic use of structure, which is to a large extent a matter of borrowing images and forms from other technical areas without seriously appraising their technical suitability, is incapable of addressing real technical problems of the type which are posed by the need for sustainability. The ideology is that of Modernism which is committed to the belief in technical progress and the continual destruction and renewal of the built environment[12]. This is a high-energy-consumption scenario which is not ecologically sound.

The benefits of new technological solutions would have to be much greater than at present for this approach to be useful. The forms of a future sustainable architecture are more likely to be evolved from the combination of innovative environmental technology with traditional building forms, which are environmentally friendly because they are adapted to local climatic conditions and are constructed in durable, locally available materials, than by transferring technology from the extremely environmentally unfriendly aerospace industry.

The second category of *structure as ornament* involves an unnecessary structural problem, created either intentionally or unintentionally, which generates the need for a spectacular response. A good example of this is found in the structure of the Centre Pompidou and concerns the way in which the floor girders are connected to the columns (Figs 7.7 and 6.7).

The rectangular cross-section of this building has three zones at every level (Fig. 7.8). There is a central main space which is flanked by two peripheral zones: on one side of the building the peripheral zone is used for a circulation system of corridors and escalators; on the other it contains services. The architects chose to use the glass wall which formed the building's envelope to delineate these zones

---

11 Chief amongst these is Richard Rogers and the arguments are set out in Rogers, *Architecture, A Modern View*, Thames and Hudson, London, 1991.

12 This is very well articulated by Charles Jencks in 'The New Moderns', AD Profile – *New Architecture: The New Moderns and The Super Moderns*, 1990.

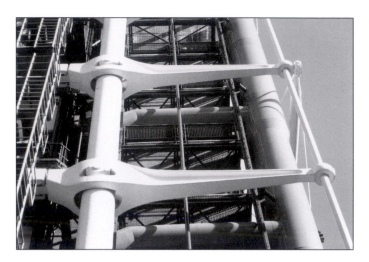

Fig. 7.7 Gerberette brackets, Centre Pompidou, Paris, France, 1978; Piano and Rogers, architects; Ove Arup & Partners, structural engineers. The floor girders are attached to the inner ends of these brackets, which pivot on hinge pins through the columns. The weights of the floors are counterbalanced by tie forces applied at the outer ends of the brackets. The arrangement sends 25% more force into the columns than would occur if the floor beams were attached to them directly. (Photo: A. Macdonald)

and placed the services and circulation zones outside the envelope. The distinction is mirrored in the structural arrangement: the main structural frames, which consist of triangulated girders spanning the central space, are linked to the perimeter columns through cantilever brackets, named 'gerberettes' after the nineteenth-century bridge engineer Heinrich Gerber, which are associated with the peripheral zones. The joints between the brackets and the main frames coincide with the building's glass wall and the spatial and structural zonings are therefore identical.

The elaborate gerberette brackets, which are major visual elements on the exterior of the building, pivot around the hinges connecting

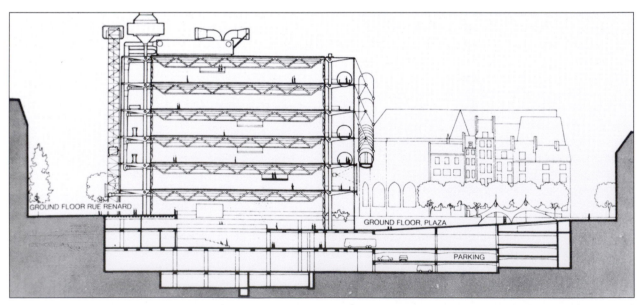

Fig. 7.8 Cross-section, Centre Pompidou, Paris, France, 1978; Piano and Rogers, architects; Ove Arup & Partners, structural engineers. The building is subdivided into three principal zones at every level and the spatial and structural arrangements correspond. The main interior spaces occupy a central zone associated with the main floor girders. The gerberette brackets define peripheral zones on either side of the building which are associated with circulation and services.

them to the columns (Fig. 7.7). The weights of the floors, which are supported on the inner ends of the brackets, are counterbalanced by downward-acting reactions at the outer ends provided by vertical tie rods linking them with the foundations. This arrangement sends 25% more force into the columns at each level than is required to support the floors. The idea of connecting the floor girders to the columns through these cantilevered brackets does not therefore make a great deal of engineering sense.

Apart from the unnecessary overloading of the columns, the brackets themselves are subjected to high levels of bending-type internal force and their design presented an interesting, if unnecessary, challenge to the engineers. The required solution to this was to give the brackets a highly complex geometry which reflected their structural function. The level of complexity could only be achieved by casting of the metal, and the idea of fabricating the brackets from cast steel, a technique which was virtually unknown in architecture at the time, was both courageous and innovative. It allowed forms to be used which were both expressive of the structural function of the brackets and which made a more efficient use of material than would have occurred had they been made from standard I-sections. According to Richard Rogers: 'We were repeating the gerberette brackets over 200 times and it was cheaper to use less steel than it was to use an I-beam. That's the argument on that I would have thought'[13].

Another advantage of casting was that it introduced an element of hand crafting into the steelwork. This was something of a preoccupation of Peter Rice, the principal structural engineer on the project who, in something of the tradition of the much earlier British Arts and Crafts Movement, believed that much of the inhumanity of Modern architecture stemmed from the fact that it was composed entirely of machine-made components.

There were therefore several agendas involved, most of them concerned with visual rather than structural considerations, and

Fig. 7.9 Lloyds headquarters building, London, UK, 1986; Richard Rogers and Partners, architects; Ove Arup & Partners, structural engineers. The building has a rectangular plan and six projecting service towers.

there is no doubt that the presence of these unusual components on the exterior of the building contributes greatly to its aesthetic success. Thus, the ingenious solution of an unnecessarily-created technical problem found architectural expression. This is the essence of this version of *structure as ornament*. Its greatest exponent has perhaps been the Spanish architect/engineer Santiago Calatrava.

A third kind of architecture which involves structure of questionable technical validity occurs in the context of a visual agenda that is incompatible with structural requirements. The Lloyds headquarters building (Fig. 7.9) in

---

13 Interview with the author, February 2000.

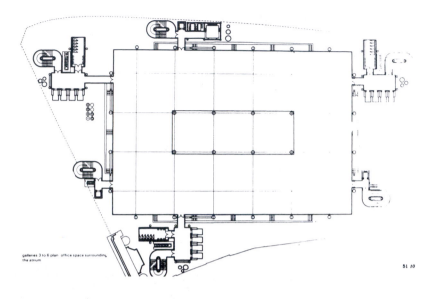

Fig. 7.10 Plan, Lloyds headquarters building, London, UK, 1986; Richard Rogers and Partners, architects; Ove Arup & Partners, structural engineers. The building has a rectangular plan with a central atrium. The structure is a reinforced concrete beam-column frame carrying a one-way-spanning floor.

Fig. 7.11 Lloyds headquarters building, London, UK, 1986; Richard Rogers and Partners, architects; Ove Arup & Partners, structural engineers. The service towers which project from the rectangular plan are one of the most distinctive features of the building.

London, by the same designers who produced the Centre Pompidou (Richard Rogers and Partners as architects and Ove Arup and Partners as structural engineers), is a good example of this.

Lloyds is a multi-storey office building with a rectangular plan (Fig. 7.10). The building has a central atrium through most levels, which converts the floor plan into a rectangular doughnut, and, as at the Centre Pompidou, services which are external to the building's envelope. At Lloyds these are placed in a series of towers which disguise the rectilinearity of the building. There are also external ducts which grip the building like the tentacles of an octopus (Fig. 7.11). The structural armature is a reinforced concrete beam-and-column framework which supports the rectangular core of the building. This forms a prominent element of the visual vocabulary but is problematic technically.

The columns are located outside the perimeter of the floor structures which they support and this has the effect of increasing the eccentricity with which load is applied to the columns – a highly undesirable consequence structurally. This solution was adopted to make the structure 'readable' (a continuing concern of Richard Rogers) by articulating the different parts as separate identifiable elements. It resulted in the floors being connected to the columns through elaborate pre-cast concrete brackets (Fig. 7.12). In this respect the Lloyds building is similar to the Centre Pompidou. An architectural idea, 'readability', created a problem which required a structural response. The pre-cast column junctions were less spectacular than the gerberettes of the Centre Pompidou, but had an equivalent function, both technically and visually.

There are, however, important differences between Pompidou and Lloyds which place them in slightly different categories so far as the relationship between structure and architecture is concerned. At Lloyds, the logic of readability was abandoned in the treatment of the underside of the exposed reinforced concrete floors. These take the shape of a rectangular doughnut in plan due to the presence of the central atrium. Structurally, they consist of primary beams, spanning between columns at the perimeter and within the atrium, which support a ribbed one-way-spanning floor system. For purely visual reasons the presence of the primary beams was suppressed and they were concealed by the square grid of the floor structure. The impression thus given is that the floors are a two-way-spanning system supported directly on the columns without primary beams. Great ingenuity was required on the part of the structural engineering team to produce a structure which had a satisfactory technical performance while at the same time appearing to be that which it was not.

This task was not made easier by another visual requirement, namely that the ribs of the floor structure should appear to be parallel-sided rather than tapered. A small amount of taper was in fact essential to allow the formwork to be extracted, but to make the ribs appear to be parallel-sided the taper was upwards rather than downwards. This meant that the formwork had to be taken out from above which eliminated the possibility of continuity between the ribs and the floor slab which they support. The benefits of composite action between the ribs and the floor slab, which normally greatly increases the efficiency

Fig. 7.12 Atrium, Lloyds headquarters building, London, UK, 1986; Richard Rogers and Partners, architects; Ove Arup & Partners, structural engineers. The columns are set outside the perimeter of the floor decks and connected to them through visually prominent pre-cast concrete brackets. The arrangement allows the structure to be easily 'read' but is far from ideal structurally. It introduces bending into the columns, which causes high concentrations of stress at the junctions.

of reinforced concrete floors, were thus foregone. The design of this structure was therefore driven almost entirely by visual considerations and a heavy penalty was paid in terms of structural efficiency.

The conclusion which may be drawn from the above examples of *structure as ornament* is that in many buildings with exposed structures the structure is technically flawed despite appearing visually interesting. This does not mean that the architects and engineers who designed these buildings were incompetent or that the buildings themselves are examples of bad architecture. It does mean, however, that in much architecture in which exposed structure is used to convey the idea of technical excellence (most of High-Tech architecture falls into this category), the forms and visual devices which have been employed are not themselves examples of technology which is appropriate to the function involved. It will remain to be seen whether these buildings stand the test of time, either physically or intellectually: the ultimate fate of many of them, despite their enjoyable qualities, may be that of the discarded toy.

7.2.3 Structure as architecture

7.2.3.1 Introduction

There have always been buildings which consisted of structure and only structure. The igloo and the tepee (see Figs 1.2 and 1.3) are examples and such buildings have, of course, existed throughout history and much of human pre-history. In the world of architectural history and criticism they are considered to be 'vernacular' rather than 'architecture'. Occasionally, they have found their way into the architectural discourse and where this has occurred it has often been due to the very large scale of the particular example. Examples are the Crystal Palace (Fig. 7.25) in the nineteenth century and the CNIT building (see Fig. 1.4) in the twentieth. These were buildings in which the limits of what was technically feasible were approached and in which no compromise with structural requirements was possible. This is a third type of relationship between structure and architecture which might be referred to as *structure without ornament*, but perhaps even more accurately as *structure as architecture*.

The limits of what is possible structurally are reached in the obvious cases of very long

spans and tall buildings. Other cases are those in which extreme lightness is desirable, for example because the building is required to be portable, or where some other technical issue is so important that it dictates the design programme.

7.2.3.2 The very long span

It is necessary to begin a discussion on long-span structures by asking the question: when is a span a long span? The answer offered here will be: when, as a consequence of the size of the span, technical considerations are placed so high on the list of architectural priorities that they significantly affect the aesthetic treatment of the building. As has already been discussed in Chapter 6, the technical problem posed by the long span is that of maintaining a reasonable balance between the load carried and the self-weight of the structure. The forms of longest-span structures are therefore those of the most efficient structure types, namely the form-active types such as the compressive vault and the tensile membrane, and the non- or semi-form-active types into which significant 'improvements' have been incorporated.

In the pre-industrial age the structural form which was used for the widest spans was the masonry vault or the dome. The only other structural material available in the pre-industrial age was timber. Due to the small size of individual timbers, any large wooden structure involved the joining together of many elements, and making joints in timber which had satisfactory structural performance was difficult. In the absence of a satisfactory jointing technology, large-scale structures in timber were not feasible in the pre-Modern world. Also, the understanding of how to produce efficient fully-triangulated trusses did not occur until the nineteenth century.

The development of reinforced concrete in the late nineteenth century allowed the extension of the maximum span which was possible with the compressive form-active type of structure. Reinforced concrete has a number of advantages over masonry, the principal one being its capability to resist tension as well as compression and its consequent ability to resist bending. The vault and the dome are, of course, compressive form-active structures, but this does not mean that they are never subjected to bending moment because the form-active shape is only valid for a specific load pattern. Structures which support buildings are subjected to variations in the load pattern, with the result that compressive form-active structures will in some circumstances become semi-form-active and be required to resist bending. If the structural material has little tensile strength, as is the case with masonry, its cross-section must be sufficiently thick to prevent the tensile bending stress from exceeding the compressive axial stress which is also present. Masonry vaults and domes must therefore be fairly thick and this compromises their efficiency. An additional complication with the use of the dome is that tensile stresses can develop in the circumferential direction near the base of the structure with the result that cracks develop. Most masonry domes are in fact reinforced to a limited extent with metal – usually in the form of iron bars – to counteract this tendency.

Because reinforced concrete can resist both tensile and bending stress, compressive form-active structures in this material can be made very much thinner than those in masonry. This allows greater efficiency, and therefore greater spans, to be achieved because the principal load on a dome or vault is the weight of the structure itself.

Another advantage of reinforced concrete is that it makes easier the adoption of 'improved' cross-sections. This technique has been used with masonry domes, however, the twin skins of Brunelleschi's dome for Florence Cathedral (Fig. 7.13)[14] being an example, but the

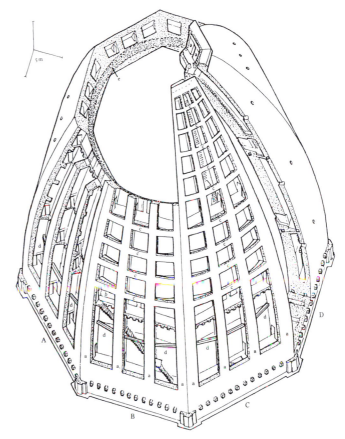

Fig. 7.13 Dome of the cathedral, Florence, Italy, 1420–36; Brunelleschi. The dome of the cathedral at Florence is a semi-form-active structure. The brickwork masonry envelope has an 'improved' cross-section and consists of inner and outer skins linked by diaphragms. An ingenious pattern of brickwork bonding was adopted to ensure satisfactory composite action. Given the span involved, and certain other constraints such as that the dome had to sit on an octagonal drum, it is difficult to imagine any other form which would have been feasible structurally. This memorable work of architecture is therefore an example of genuine 'high tech'. The overall form was determined from structural considerations and not compromised for visual effect. (Drawing: R. J. Mainstone)

mouldability of reinforced concrete greatly extended this potential for increasing the efficiency with which a dome or vault can resist bending moment caused by semi-form-active load patterns.

Among the earliest examples of the use of reinforced concrete for vaulting on a large scale are the airship hangars for Orly Airport in

---

14 The twin skin arrangement may not have been adopted for structural reasons. An interesting speculation is whether Brunelleschi, who was a brilliant technologist, may have had an intuitive understanding of the improved structural performance which results from a two-skin arrangement.

Fig. 7.14 Airship Hangars, Orly Airport, France, 1921; Eugène Freyssinet, structural engineer. The skin of this compressive form-active vault has a corrugated cross-section which allows efficient resistance to secondary bending moment. The form adopted was fully justified given the span involved and was almost entirely determined from structural considerations.

Fig. 7.15 Palazzetto dello Sport, Rome, Italy, 1960; Pier Luigi Nervi, architect/engineer. This is another example of a building with a form determined solely from structural requirements. The compressive form-active dome is a composite of *in situ* and pre-cast reinforced concrete and has an 'improved' corrugated cross-section. (Photo: British Cement Association)

Paris by Eugène Freyssinet (Fig. 7.14). A corrugated cross-section was used in these buildings to improve the bending resistance of the vaults. Other masters of this type of

structure in the twentieth century were Pier Luigi Nervi, Eduardo Torroja and Félix Candela. Nervi's structures (Fig. 7.15) are especially interesting because he developed a system of construction which involved the use of pre-cast permanent formwork in ferro-cement, a type of concrete made from very fine aggregate and which could be moulded into extremely slender and delicate shapes. The elimination of much of the temporary formwork and the ease with which the ferro-cement could be moulded into 'improved' cross-sections of complex geometry, allowed long-span structures of great sophistication to be built relatively economically. The final dome or vault consisted of a composite structure of *in-situ* concrete and ferro-cement formwork.

Other notable examples of twentieth-century compressive form-active structures are the CNIT building in Paris by Nicolas Esquillan (see Fig. 1.4) and the roof of the Smithfield Poultry Market in London by R. S. Jenkins of Ove Arup and Partners (Fig. 7.16).

Compressive form-active structures are also produced in metal, usually in the form of lattice arches or vaults, to achieve very long spans. Some of the most spectacular of these are also among the earliest, the train shed at St Pancras Station in London (1868) by William Barlow and R. M. Ordish (span 73 m) (Fig. 7.51) and the structure of the Galerie des Machines for the Paris Exhibition of 1889, by Contamin and Dutert (span 114 m) being notable examples. The subject has been well reviewed by Wilkinson[15]. This tradition continues in the present day and notable recent examples are the International Rail Terminal at Waterloo Station, London, by Nicholas Grimshaw & Partners with YRM Anthony Hunt Associates (Fig. 7.17) and the design for the Kansai Airport building for Osaka, Japan by Renzo Piano with Ove Arup and Partners.

Cable-network structures are another group whose appearance is distinctive because

15 *Op. cit.*

Fig. 7.16 Smithfield Poultry Market, London, UK; Ove Arup & Partners, structural engineers. The architecture here is dominated by the semi-form-active shell structure which forms the roof of the building. Its adoption was justified by the span of around 60 m. The elliptical paraboloid shape was selected rather than a fully form-active geometry because it could be easily described mathematically, which simplified both the design and the construction. (Photo: John Maltby Ltd)

Fig. 7.17 International Rail Terminal, Waterloo Station, London, UK, 1992; Nicholas Grimshaw & Partners, architects; YRM Anthony Hunt Associates, structural engineers. This building is part of a continuing tradition of long-span structures for railway stations. The design contains a number of innovatory features, most notably the use of tapering steel sub-elements. (Photo: J. Reid and J. Peck)

Fig. 7.18 David S. Ingalls ice hockey rink, Yale, USA, 1959; Eero Saarinen, architect; Fred Severud, structural engineer. A combination of compressive form-active arches and a tensile form-active cable network was used in this long-span building. The architecture is totally dominated by the structural form.

technical considerations have been allocated a very high priority, due to the need to achieve a long span or a very lightweight structure. They are tensile form-active structures in which a very high level of efficiency is achieved. Their principal application has been as the roof structures for large single-volume buildings such as sports arenas. The ice hockey arena at Yale by Eero Saarinen (Fig. 7.18) and the cable-network structures of Frei Otto (see Fig. i) are typical examples.

In these buildings the roof envelope is an anticlastic double-curved surface[16]: two opposite curvatures exist at every location. The surface is formed by two sets of cables, one conforming to each of the constituent directions of curvature, an arrangement which allows the cables to be pre-stressed against

---

16 The terms anticlastic and synclastic describe different families of curved surface. An anticlastic surface is described by two sets of curves acting in opposite directions. The canopy of the Olympic stadium at Munich (Fig. i) is an example. Synclastic surfaces are also doubly curved but with the describing curves acting in the same direction. The shell roof of the Smithfield Poultry market (Fig. 7.16) is an example of this type.

each other. The opposing directions of curvature give the structure the ability to tolerate reversals of load (necessary to resist wind loading without gross distortion in shape) and the pre-stressing enables minimisation of the movement which occurs under variations in load (necessary to prevent damage to the roof cladding).

In the 1990s, a new generation of mast-supported synclastic cable networks was developed. The principal advantage of these over the earlier anticlastic forms was that, due to the greater simplicity of the form, the manufacture of the cladding was made easier.

The Millennium Dome in London (Fig. 7.19), which is not of course a dome in the structural sense, is perhaps the best known of these. In this building a dome-shaped cable network is supported on a ring of 24 masts. The overall diameter of the building is 358 m but the maximum span is approximately 225 m, which is the diameter of the ring described by the 24 masts. The size of the span makes the use of a complex form-active structure entirely justified. The cable network to which the cladding is attached consists of a series of radial cables, in pairs, which span 25 m between nodes supported by hanger cables connecting them to the tops of the masts. The nodes are also connected by circumferential cables which provide stability. The downward curving radial cables are pre-stressed against the hanger cables and this makes them almost straight and converts the surface of the dome into a series of facetted panels. It is this characteristic which simplifies the fabrication of the cladding. In fact, being tensile form-active elements, the radial cables are slightly curved, and this curvature had to be allowed for in the design of the cladding, but the overall geometry is nevertheless considerably less complex than an anticlastic surface. The cladding fabric of the Millennium Dome is PTFE-coated glass fibre.

The few examples of cable networks illustrated here demonstrate that, although this type of structure is truly form-active with a shape which is dependent on the pattern of applied load, the designer can exert

Fig. 7.19 Millennium Dome, London, UK, 1999; Richard Rogers and Partners, architects; Buro Happold, structural engineers. This is mast-supported, dome-shaped cable network with a diameter of 358 m. The use of a tensile form-active structure is fully justified for structures of this size.

considerable influence on the overall form through the choice of support conditions and surface type. The cable network can be supported either on a configuration of semi-form-active arches or on a series of masts; it can also be either synclastic or anticlastic and the configurations which are adopted for these influence the overall appearance of the building.

Judged by the criteria outlined in Section 6.3, most of the form-active vaulted and cable structures are not without technical shortcomings. They are difficult to design and build and, due to their low mass, provide poor thermal barriers. In addition, the durability of these structures, especially the cable networks, is lower than that of most conventional building envelopes. Acceptance of these deficiencies is justified, however, in the interests of achieving the high levels of structural efficiency required to produce large

spans. In the cases described here the compromise which has been reached is satisfactory, given the spans involved and the uses for which the buildings were designed.

All of the long-span buildings considered here may therefore be regarded as true 'high-tech' architecture. They are state-of-the-art examples of structural technology employed to achieve some of the largest span enclosures in existence. The technology employed was necessary to achieve the spans involved and the resulting forms have been given minimal stylistic treatment.

7.2.3.3 *Very tall buildings*
In the search for the truly high-tech building, which is another way of thinking of the category *structure as architecture*, the skyscraper is worthy of careful consideration. From a structural point of view two problems are posed by the very high building: one is the

provision of adequate vertical support and the other is the difficulty of resisting high lateral loading, including the dynamic effect of wind. So far as vertical support is concerned, the strength required of the columns or walls is greatest at the base of the building, where the need for an excessively large volume of structure is a potential problem. In the days before the introduction of iron and steel this was a genuine difficulty which placed a limit on the possible height of structures. The problem was solved by the introduction of steel framing. Columns are loaded axially, and so long as the storey height is low enough to maintain the slenderness ratio[17] at a reasonably low level and thus inhibit buckling, the strength of the material is such that excessive volume of structure does not occur within the maximum practical height limits imposed by other, non-structural constraints.

The need to increase the level of vertical support towards the base of a tall building has rarely been expressed architecturally. In many skyscrapers the apparent size of the vertical structure – the columns and walls – is identical throughout the entire height of the building. There have, of course, been many technical innovations in connection with aspects of the support of gravitational load in high buildings. In particular, as was pointed out by Billington[18], changes in the relationship between the vertical and horizontal structural elements have led to the creation of larger column-free spaces in the interiors. These innovations have, however, found very limited architectural expression.

The need to accommodate wind loading as opposed to gravitational loads has had a greater effect on the aesthetics of very tall buildings. As with vertical support elements, in the majority of skyscrapers the architect has been able to choose not to express the

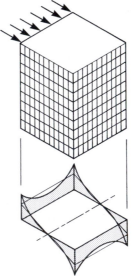

17 See Macdonald, Angus J., *Structural Design for Architecture*, Architectural Press, Oxford, 1997, Appendix 2, for an explanation of slenderness ratio.

18 Billington, D. P., *The Tower and the Bridge*, Basic Books, New York, 1983.

Fig. 7.20 World Trade Centre, New York, USA, 1973; Minoru Yamasaki, architect; Skilling, Helle, Christiansen & Robertson, structural engineers. The closely-spaced columns on the exteriors of these buildings are structural and form a 'framed-tube' which provides efficient resistance to lateral load. In response to lateral load the building acts as a vertical cantilever with a hollow box cross-section. This is an example of a structural system, not compromised for visual reasons, exerting a major influence on the appearance of the building. (Photo: R. J. Mainstone)

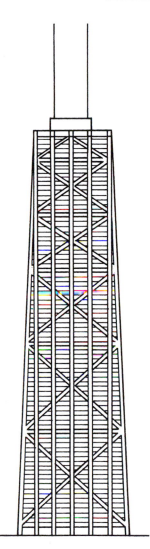

Fig. 7.21 John Hancock Building, Chicago, USA, 1969; Skidmore, Owings and Merrill, architects and structural engineers. The trussed-tube structure here forms a major component of the visual vocabulary. (Photo: Chris Smallwood)

bracing structure so that, although many of these buildings are innovative in a structural sense, this is not visually obvious. The very tallest buildings, however, have been designed to behave as single vertical cantilevers with the structure concentrated on the exterior; in these cases the expression of the structural action was unavoidable.

The framed- and trussed-tube configurations[19] (Figs 7.20 and 7.21) are examples of structural arrangements which allow tall buildings to behave as vertical

19 See Schueller, W., *High Rise Building Structures*, John Wiley, London, 1977, for an explanation of bracing systems for very tall buildings.

93

Fig. 7.22 Sears Tower, Chicago, USA, 1974; Skidmore, Owings and Merrill, architects and structural engineers. This building, which is currently the tallest in the world, is subdivided internally by a cruciform arrangement of 'walls' of closely spaced columns which enhance its resistance to wind loading. This structural layout is expressed in the exterior form.

cantilevers in response to wind loads. In both cases the building is treated as a hollow tube, a non-form-active element with an 'improved' cross-section, in its resistance to lateral loading. The tube is formed by concentrating the vertical structure at the perimeter of the plan. The floors span from this to a central services core which provides vertical support but does not normally contribute to the resistance of wind load.

Such buildings are usually given a square plan. With the wind blowing parallel to one of the faces, the columns on the windward and leeward walls act as tensile and compression flanges respectively of the cantilever cross-section, while the two remaining external walls form a shear link between these. In the case of the framed tube, of which the World Trade Centre buildings in New York by Minoru Yamasaki (Fig. 7.20) are examples, the shear connection is provided by rigid frame action between the columns and the very short beams which link them. In trussed-tube structures, such as the John Hancock Building in Chicago by Skidmore, Owings and Merrill (Fig. 7.21), the shear connection is provided by diagonal bracing elements. Because in each of these cases the special structural configuration which was adopted to provide resistance to lateral load resulted in the structure being concentrated in the outer walls of the building, the structure contributed significantly to, and indeed determined, the visual expression of the architecture. Hal Iyengar, chief structural engineer in the Chicago office of Skidmore, Owings and Merrill described the relationship thus:

> '... the characteristics of the project create a unique structure and then the architect capitalises on it. That's exactly what happened in the Hancock building.'[20]

A development of the cantilever tube idea is the so-called 'bundled-tube' – a system in which the shear connection between the windward and leeward walls is made by internal walls as well as those on the sides of the building. This results in a square grid arrangement of closely spaced 'walls' of columns. The Sears Tower in Chicago, also by Skidmore, Owings and Merrill (Fig. 7.22), has this type of structure which is expressed architecturally, in this case by varying the heights of each of the compartments created by the structural grid. The structural system is therefore a significant contributor to the external appearance of this building.

Thus, among very high buildings some examples of *structure as architecture* may be found. These are truly high tech in the sense that, because the limits of technical possibility have been approached, structural considerations have been given a high priority

in the design – to the extent that the appearance of the building has been significantly affected by them.

7.2.3.4 *The lightweight building*

The situation in which saving in weight is an essential requirement is another scenario which causes technical considerations to be allocated a very high priority in the design of a building. This often comes about when the building is required to be portable. The backpacker's tent – an extreme example of the need to minimise weight in a portable building – has already been mentioned. Portability requires not only that the building be light but also that it be demountable – another purely technical consideration. In such a case the resulting building form is determined almost entirely by technical criteria.

As has been repeatedly emphasised, the most efficient type of structure is the form-active one and the traditional solution to the problem of portable buildings is, of course, the tent, which is a tensile form-active structure. The tent also has the advantage of being easy to demount and collapse into a small volume, which compressive form-active structures have not, due to the rigidity which they must possess in order to resist compression. This solution has therefore been widely used for temporary or portable buildings throughout history and is found in a very wide range of situations from the portable houses of nomadic peoples to the temporary buildings of industrialised societies, whether in the form of tents for recreation or temporary buildings for other purposes. Figure 7.23 shows an example of state-of-the-art engineering used for a building to house a temporary exhibition – another example of truly high-tech architecture.

Although the field of temporary buildings remains dominated by the tent in all its forms, the compressive form-active structure has also been used for such purposes. A late-twentieth-century example was the building designed by Renzo Piano for the travelling exhibition of

20 Conversation with Janice Tuchman reported in Thornton, C., Tomasetti, R., Tuchman, J. and Joseph, L., *Exposed Structure in Building Design*, McGraw-Hill, New York, 1993.

Fig. 7.23   Tent structure for temporary exhibition building, Hyde Park, London, UK; Ove Arup & Partners, structural engineers. Lightweight, portable buildings may be considered as examples of genuine 'high-tech' architecture in any age because the forms adopted are determined almost entirely from structural and constructional considerations.

Fig. 7.24   Building for IBM Europe travelling exhibition; Renzo Piano, architect/engineer; Ove Arup & Partners, structural engineers. This building consists of a semi-form-active compressive vault. The 'improved' cross-section of the membrane is achieved with a highly sophisticated combination of laminated timber and plastic – each is a material which offers high strength for its weight. Technical considerations reign supreme here to produce a portable, lightweight building.

IBM Europe (Fig. 7.24). This consisted of a semi-form-active vault which was 'improved' by triangulation. The sub-elements were laminated beechwood struts and ties linked by polycarbonate pyramids. These elements were bolted together using aluminium connectors. The structure combined lightness of weight, which was achieved through the use of low-density materials and an efficient structural geometry, with ease of assembly – the two essential requirements of a portable building. No technical compromises were made for visual or stylistic reasons.

7.2.3.5 *Special requirements*

Other forms of special requirement besides the need for a lightweight structure can result in structural issues being accorded the highest

Fig. 7.25 Crystal Palace, London, UK, 1851; Joseph Paxton, architect/engineer. The Crystal Palace was a truly high-tech building and an inspiration to generations of modern architects. Unlike many twentieth-century buildings to which the label High Tech has been applied, it was at the forefront of what was technically possible at the time. The major decisions affecting the form of the building were taken for technical reasons and were not compromised for visual or stylistic effect. The building has technical shortcomings, such as the poor durability of the many joints in the external skin, but in the context of a temporary building it was appropriate that these were given a low priority.

priority in the design of a building to the point at which they exert a dominating influence on its form. A classic example of this from the nineteenth century was the Crystal Palace in London (Fig. 7.25) which was built to house the Great Exhibition of 1851.

The problem which Joseph Paxton, the designer of the Crystal Palace, was required to solve was that of producing a building which could be manufactured and erected very quickly (nine months elapsed between the original sketch design and the completion of the building) and which could subsequently be dismantled and re-erected elsewhere. Given the immense size of the building, comparable with that of a Gothic cathedral, the technical problem was indeed formidable. Paxton's solution was to build a glasshouse – a glass envelope supported by an exposed structure of iron and timber. It is difficult to

imagine any other contemporary structural solution which could have met the design requirements. Possibly a series of very large tents would have sufficed – there was in existence at the time a fairly large canvas- and rope-making capability associated with shipbuilding and a tradition of large tent manufacture. Tents would not, however, have provided the lofty interior which was desirable to display adequately the latest products of industry. The Crystal Palace not only solved the problem of the large and lofty enclosure; it was itself a demonstration of the capabilities of the latest industrial processes and techniques of mass production.

The technology used for the building was developed by the builders of glasshouses for horticulture, of whom Paxton was perhaps the most innovative. It contained much that the enthusiast of structural engineering and industrial technology could enjoy. The post-and-beam structure was appropriate for the spans and loads involved. Form-active arches were used as the horizontal elements in the post-and-beam format to span the large central 'nave' and 'transepts', and non-form-active, straight girders with triangulated 'improved' profiles formed the shorter spans of the flanking 'aisles'. The glazing conformed to a ridge-and-furrow arrangement, which was designed originally in connection with horticultural glasshouses to improve the daylight-penetration characteristics – it provided some shade during the hours around mid-day when the sun was high in the sky but admitted more light in the early morning and late evening. Although this characteristic was not particularly important in the case of the Crystal Palace, the arrangement enhanced the structural performance by giving the glass cladding a structurally 'improved', corrugated cross-section. Many other examples of good technology were features of the building – one of which was that the secondary beams supporting the glazing served also as rainwater guttering to conduct the run-off to the columns whose circular hollow cross-sections, as well as having ideal structural shapes for compression elements, allowed them to

function as drain pipes. Another example was that much of the structure was discontinuous and this, through the elimination of the 'lack-of-fit' problem (see Appendix 3), together with the very large degree of component repetition, facilitated both the rapid manufacture of the elements by mass-production techniques and the very fast assembly of the building on site.

The building was therefore at the forefront of contemporary technology – a genuine example of a high-tech building – and was ideally suited to its purpose, which was to house a temporary exhibition. The technical shortcomings of the arrangement – the lack of thermal insulation, the susceptibility to leaks at the many joints in the cladding and the questionable long-term durability of the structure and of the cladding joints – were not significant in this context, as they would have been in a permanent building.

Many twentieth-century Modern architects have been inspired by the glass-clad framework of the Crystal Palace. As was the case with the later examples of 'technology transfer' already mentioned, although with some notable exceptions such as the Patera Building described below, it was the imagery rather than the technical reality which was attractive to them.

Fig. 7.26 Patera Building; Michael Hopkins, architect; Anthony Hunt Associates, structural engineers. The building consists of a lightweight steel framework which supports an insulated cladding system and fully glazed end walls. The principal structural elements are external and the purlins and cladding rails are located within the cladding zone to give a very clean interior. (Photo: Anthony Hunt Associates)

The Patera Building, by Michael Hopkins with Tony Hunt as structural engineer (Fig 7.26) has been directly compared to the Crystal Palace because its design was also based on the principle of pre-fabrication. The project was an attempt to address the problem of the poor architectural quality of most industrial estates by producing a building system which would be economic, flexible and stylish and linking this to a development company which would act as the co-ordinator of industrial estates. The development company would acquire land, design a layout of building plots and install infrastructure. Individual tenant clients would then have buildings tailor-made to their requirements within a consistent style offered by a building system. The buildings would, in effect, be industrial apartments capable of being adapted to different client requirements and offered for rent for varying lengths of tenure to suit clients' needs.

The principal hardware element in the concept was a basic building shell which could be erected and fitted out quickly to meet the needs of an individual tenant and then easily adapted to suit the requirements of subsequent tenants. It was envisaged that the scale of the operation would allow the building to be treated as an industrial product; it would be developed and tested in prototype form and subsequently manufactured in sufficient numbers to cover its development costs.

It was envisaged that the erection of the building would occur in three phases. The first of these was the laying of a rectangular foundation and ground-floor slab in which services would be incorporated. This was the interface between the superstructure and the site and rendered the building non-site-specific. The building could be built anywhere that this standard rectangular slab could be laid. The second stage was the erection of the superstructure, a shell of cladding, incorporating trunking for electrical and telephone services, supported on a steel framework. The third stage was the subdivision and fitting out of the interior to meet specific client requirements.

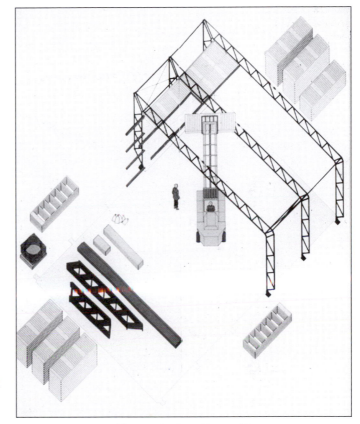

Fig. 7.27   Patera Building; Michael Hopkins, architect; Anthony Hunt Associates, structural engineers. Technical considerations, such as the need for containerisation and for simple assembly with a fork-lift truck exerted a major influence on the design. (Photo: Anthony Hunt Associates)

The structure of the building consisted of a series of triangulated portal frameworks which spanned 13.2 m across the building, linked by rectangular-hollow-section purlins and cladding rails spaced 1.2 m apart and spanning 3.6 m between the main frames. The main frameworks were ingeniously designed to meet exacting performance requirements which called for a structure that would be of stylish appearance with, for ease of containerisation, no element longer than 6.75 m and, for ease of construction, no element heavier than could be lifted by a fork-lift truck (Fig. 7.27). To meet

Fig. 7.28 Patera Building; Michael Hopkins, architect; Anthony Hunt Associates, structural engineers. The ingenious use of pin connections and cast nodes allowed a fully rigid joint to be made between the principal elements which could be easily assembled. (Photo: Anthony Hunt Associates)

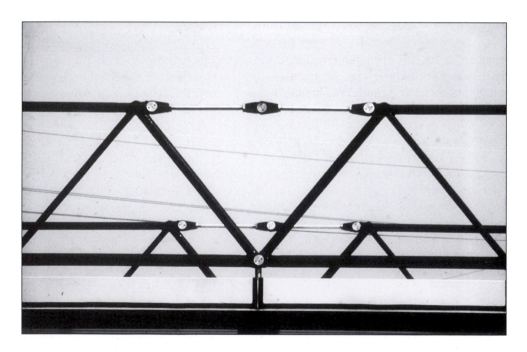

Fig. 7.29 Patera Building. The mid-span joint in the primary structure has a three-hinge tension-only link. Under gravitational load the latter collapses and the joint as a whole behaves as a hinge. Under wind uplift the tension-only link comes into play and the connection becomes rigid. The device maintains the laterally-restrained lower booms of the structure in compression under all conditions of load. (Photo: Anthony Hunt Associates)

these requirements a hybrid 2-hinge/3-hinge portal framework was chosen. The inherent efficiency of the semi-form-active arrangement, together with the full triangulation of the elements and the relatively small ratio of span to depth that was adopted, allowed very slender circular-hollow-section sub-elements to be used. Each portal consisted of two horizontal and two vertical sub-units which were pre-fabricated by welding. Cast-steel jointing components allowed the use of very precise pin-type site connections and these were cleverly arranged at the junction between the horizontal and vertical elements to provide a rigid connection there (Fig. 7.28).

The hybrid 2-hinge/3-hinge arrangement was adopted to eliminate the need for additional lateral bracing of the compression side of the structure by ensuring that the inner booms of the main elements, which were restrained laterally by the cladding, remained in compression under all conditions of loading. The key to this behaviour was an ingenious 3-pin tension-only link between the top elements of the portal at the central joint (Fig. 7.29). Under gravitational load, this was subjected to compression and collapsed to produce a hinge joint between the main elements at the mid-span position which ensured that compression was concentrated in the inner booms of the frame. If load reversal occurred due to wind uplift, reversal of stress within the structure did not occur because the tension-only link now became part of the structure and converted the main frame to a 2-hinge arrangement due to the mid-span joint between the horizontal elements becoming rigid. This meant that the laterally-restrained inner boom remained in compression and that most of the outer boom continued to be subjected only to tension. The need for lateral restraint for the outer booms was therefore eliminated under all conditions of load.

The Patera building is therefore an example of architecture resulting from a skilful technical solution to a set of very particular requirements. In this respect it is similar to the Crystal Palace.

7.2.3.6 *Conclusion*

In most of the cases described in this section the buildings have consisted of little other than a structure, the form of which was determined by purely technical criteria. The inherent architectural delight therefore consisted of an appreciation of 'pure' structural form. These truly high-tech structure types, especially the long-span, form-active structures, are considered by many to be beautiful, highly satisfying built forms.

Billington[21] goes so far as to argue that they may be considered to be examples of an art form and this issue has been discussed more recently by Holgate[22]. It is questionable, however, although it may not be important, whether a shape which has been evolved from purely technical considerations can be considered to be a work of art, however beautiful it may appear to those with the technical knowledge to appreciate it.

7.2.4 Structure as form generator/structure accepted

The terms *structure as form generator* and *structure accepted* are used here to describe a relationship between structure and architecture in which structural requirements are allowed to influence strongly the forms of buildings even though the structure itself is not necessarily exposed. In this type of relationship the configuration of elements which is most sensible structurally is accepted and the architecture accommodated to it. The reason why two cases are distinguished is that the closeness of the link between the architectural and the structural agendas is subject to considerable variation. Sometimes it is very positive, with the form-generating possibilities of structure being used to contribute to an architectural style. Alternatively, even though the overall form of a building may have been determined largely to satisfy structural requirements, the architectural interest may lie elsewhere.

The vaulted structures of Roman antiquity are an example of the first of these possibilities. The large interior spaces of the basilicas and bath houses of Imperial Rome, which are one of the chief glories of the architecture of the period and which are among the largest interiors in Western architecture, were roofed by vaults and domes

21 Billington, D. P., *Robert Maillart*, MIT Press, Cambridge, MA, 1989.

22 See Holgate, A., *The Art in Structural Design*, Clarendon Press, Oxford, 1986 and Holgate, A., *Aesthetics of Built Form*, Oxford University Press, Oxford, 1992.

Fig. 7.30 The Pantheon, Rome, 2nd century AD. The hemispherical concrete dome is supported on a cylindrical drum also of concrete. Both have thick cross-sections which have been 'improved' by the use of coffers or voids of various types and these technical devices have been incorporated into the visual scheme of the interior.

Fig. 7.31 The Basilica of Constantine, Rome, 4th century AD. The vaulted roof of the principal internal volume is supported on very thick walls from which large voids with vaulted ceilings have been extracted to reduce the volume of structural material required. These have been used to create variety in the disposition of internal volumes. As at the Pantheon the technical and visual programmes of the architecture have been brilliantly combined.

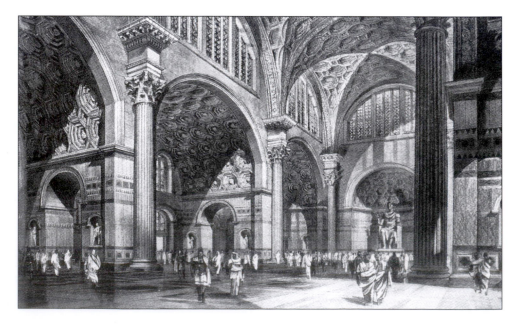

Fig. 7.32 Construction system of Roman vault. The largest interiors in Rome were constructed in unreinforced concrete which was placed in a thin skin of brickwork which acted as permanent formwork. The structural armature was then faced in marble to create a sumptuous interior. Although structural requirements dictated the overall form of the building, no part of the structure was visible.

of masonry or unreinforced concrete (Figs 7.30 to 7.32). The absence at the period of a strong structural material which could withstand tension dictated that compressive form-active structures be adopted to achieve the large spans involved. Lofty interiors of impressive grandeur were created by placing the vaults and domes on top of high walls which were given great thickness so as to accommodate the lateral thrusts produced at the wall-heads.

The Roman architects and engineers quickly appreciated that the walls did not have to be solid and a system of voided walls was developed which allowed a large overall thickness to be achieved using a minimum volume of material. The coffering on the undersides of vaults and domes was a similar device for reducing the volume and therefore weight of material involved. The walls of the main spaces in these vaulted structures are semi-form-active elements with 'improved' cross-sections. They carry axial load due to the weights of the vaults which they support and bending moments caused by the lateral thrusts of the vaults.

(a)

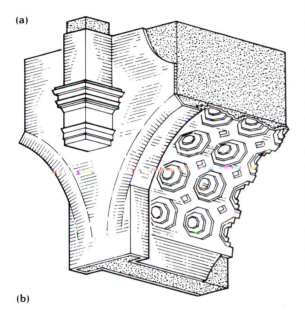

(b)

Both the voiding of the walls and the coffering of the vaults were used by the architects of Imperial Rome to create a distinctive architecture of the interior. The Pantheon in Rome (Fig. 7.30) is one of the best examples. In this building the pattern of the coffering on the underside of the dome helps to increase the apparent size of the interior and the voids and recesses in the walls of the drum which supports the dome create an illusion of the walls dissolving so that the dome appears to float above the ground.

Such techniques were further developed in the designs for bath houses and basilicas (Fig. 7.31). Interiors were created in which the possibilities offered by the structural system were fully exploited to produce spaces of great interest and variety. The device of the transverse groined vault was also used in these buildings – again principally for a technical, though not structural, reason. This was adopted in order to create flat areas of wall at high level which could be pierced by clerestory windows admitting light into what would otherwise have been dark interiors.

The vaulted structures of Imperial Rome are therefore buildings in which features which were necessary for structural reasons were incorporated into the aesthetic programme of the architecture. This was not celebration of technology but rather the imaginative exploitation of technical necessity.

Many twentieth-century architects attempted to produce a modern architecture in which the same principles were followed. One of the most enthusiastic exponents of the acceptance of structure as a generator of form was Le Corbusier, and the structural technology which he favoured was that of the non-form-active reinforced concrete flat slab, capable of spanning simultaneously in two directions and of cantilevering beyond perimeter columns. The structural action was well expressed in his famous drawing (Fig. 7.33) and the architectural opportunities which it made possible were summarised by Le

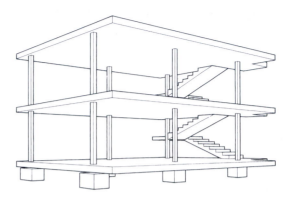

Fig. 7.33 The advantages of the structural continuity afforded by reinforced concrete are admirably summarised in the structural armature of Le Corbusier's Domino House of 1914. Thin two-way spanning slabs are supported directly on a grid of columns. The stairs provide bracing in the two principal directions.

Corbusier in his 'five points of a new architecture'[23].

This approach was used by Le Corbusier in the design of most of his buildings. The archetype is perhaps the Villa Savoye (Fig. 7.34), a building of prime importance in the development of the visual vocabulary of twentieth-century Modernism. As in Roman antiquity, the structure here is not so much celebrated as accepted and its associated opportunities exploited. Later buildings by Le Corbusier, such as the Unité d'Habitation at Marseilles or the monastery of La Tourette near Lyon, show a similar combination of structural and aesthetic programmes.

The 'Modernistic' (as opposed to Modern – see Huxtable[24]) skyscrapers which were constructed in the 1920s and 1930s in the USA, such as the Chrysler (Fig. 7.35) and Empire State buildings, are further examples of the adoption but not expression of a new structural technology – in this case that of the multi-storey steel frame. Although the architectural treatment of these buildings was

23 Le Corbusier, *Five Points Towards a New Architecture*, Paris, 1926.

24 Huxtable, A. L., *The Tall Building Reconsidered: The Search for a Skyscraper Style*, Pantheon Books, New York, 1984.

Fig. 7.34 Villa Savoye, Poissy, France, 1931; architect, Le Corbusier. The reinforced concrete structural armature of this building has, to a large extent, determined its overall form. Many other factors connected to Le Corbusier's search for a visual vocabulary appropriate to the 'machine age' contributed to the final appearance of the building, however. (Photo: Andrew Gilmour)

more conventional than those by Le Corbusier, making use of a pre-existing architectural vocabulary, they were nevertheless novel forms which owed their originality to the structural technology upon which they depended.

Another example of an early-twentieth-century building in which an innovative structure was employed, although not expressed in an overt way, was the Highpoint 1 building in London by Berthold Lubetkin and Ove Arup (Fig. 7.36). Here the structure was a 'continuous', post-and-beam arrangement of reinforced concrete walls and slabs. There were no beams and few columns and therein lay one of its innovatory aspects. The system offered great planning freedom: where openings were required, the walls above acted as beams. The level of structural efficiency was modest but was entirely appropriate for the spans involved, and other aspects of the structure, such as its durability, were also highly satisfactory. The method of construction was also original. The structure was cast on site on a reusable, moveable system of wooden formwork – also designed by Arup – and the building represented, therefore, an harmonious fusion of new architectural ideas with structural and constructional innovations. The architectural language used was discreet, however, and made no grand statement of these innovative technical features.

Fig. 7.35 Chrysler Building, New York, USA, 1930; William Van Allen, architect. Although the overall forms of Modernistic skyscrapers such as the Chrysler Building are determined by the steel frame structure the visual treatment is not. (Photo: Petra Hodgson)

(a)　　　　　　　　　　　　　　　　　　　　　**(b)**

Fig. 7.36　Highpoint 1, London, UK, 1938; Berthold Lubetkin, architect; Ove Arup, structural engineer. The structure of this building is of reinforced concrete which lends itself to a rectilinear form. The visual treatment was as much influenced by stylistic ideas of what was visually appropriate for a modern architecture as it was by technical factors connected with the structure. (Photo: A. F. Kersting)

Fig. 7.37　Willis, Faber and Dumas Office, Ipswich, UK, 1974; Foster Associates, architects; Anthony Hunt Associates, structural engineers. This building may be considered to be a late Modern equivalent of the Villa Savoye (Fig. 7.34). The relationship between structure, space planning and visual treatment is similar in both buildings. (Photo: John Donat)

A late-twentieth-century example of the positive acceptance rather than the expression of structural technology is found in the Willis, Faber and Dumas building in Ipswich, UK by Foster Associates (Fig. 7.37) with the structural engineer Tony Hunt. The structure is of the same basic type as that in Le Corbusier's drawing (Fig. 7.33) and its capabilities were fully exploited in the creation of the curvilinear plan, the provision of large wall-free spaces in the interior and the cantilevering of the floor slabs beyond the perimeter columns. The building has a roof garden and free non-structural treatment of both elevation and plan and it therefore conforms to the requirements of Le Corbusier's 'five points'.

Another example by Foster and Hunt is the pilot head office for IBM UK at Cosham (Fig. 7.38). This was intended to serve as a temporary UK main office for the IBM company and was located on a site adjacent to one on which a permanent headquarters building for IBM UK was already under construction. When the design was commissioned, IBM, in common with many rapidly-expanding

companies at the time, was making significant use of clusters of timber-framed portable buildings and envisaged that this type of accommodation would be the most suitable for the temporary head office. Foster Associates were instructed to report on the most suitable of the proprietary systems then available and to advise on the disposition of the buildings on the site. This possibility was indeed considered, but the solution which Foster recommended was that of a custom-designed building based on lightweight industrialised components, and it was this scheme that was finally executed.

Due to the need to compete with the portable building alternative on cost and speed of erection, and due to the fact that the ground conditions were poor because the site was a former land-fill rubbish tip, technical considerations exerted a major influence on the design. The design of the structure was particularly crucial to the success of the project. Tony Hunt considered using long piles (40 ft) to reach firm strata, but this would have meant reducing the number of separate

Fig. 7.38 IBM pilot head office, Cosham, UK, 1973; Foster Associates, architects; Anthony Hunt Associates, structural engineers. Intended as temporary accommodation, Foster and Hunt provided a stylish building for the same cost and within the same time-scale as those of a cluster of temporary buildings, which is what the client originally envisaged. The form adopted was to a large extent dictated by structural requirements. (Photo: Anthony Hunt Associates)

Fig. 7.39 IBM pilot head office, Cosham, UK, 1973; Foster Associates, architects; Anthony Hunt Associates, structural engineers. The structure was a steel framework with lightweight triangulated beam elements. These created a combined structural and services zone, at roof level which was essential to achieve the required flexibility in the use of the interior. (Photo: Anthony Hunt Associates)

foundations to a minimum and the resulting long-span structure would have been slow to erect and expensive to produce. The alternative was to use a short-span structure in conjunction with a rigid raft foundation that would 'float' on the low-bearing-capacity substrata. A number of such systems were considered. The favoured system was configured with lightweight triangulated girders which created a combined structure and services zone at roof level which was crucial to the provision of the required flexibility in the use of space (Fig. 7.39).

The IBM pilot head office was remarkably successful in almost every respect. It provided the client with a distinctive, stylish building which was enjoyable in use for all grades of employee, and which was undoubtedly a preferable solution to the client's requirements than the assemblage of proprietary portable buildings that they had originally envisaged. A measure of the success of the building was that, although it had been intended as temporary accommodation to last for a period of three to four years, it was retained by the company, following the completion of the permanent head office, and converted for use as an independent research unit.

The choice of the lightweight steelwork system was crucial to the success of the IBM building. It was a straightforward assemblage of proprietary Metsec components. This was both inexpensive and allowed the structure to be rapidly erected on site using no plant larger than a fork-lift truck. The resulting speed and economy was what made the building competitive with the alternatives. The structure does not form a significant visual element as most of it is concealed behind finishing elements. It did, however, exert a major influence on the final form of the building. This is therefore *structure as form generator* rather than *structure as architecture*.

The architectural interest in the IBM building lies in the stylish way in which the various components, particularly the finishing components such as the glass external wall, were detailed. Thus, although the need to produce a light and economical structure which could be erected very quickly played a significant role in determining the overall form of the building, the relationship between structure and architecture is here much less deterministic than was the case with the vaulted buildings of Roman antiquity or the Willis, Faber and Dumas building, where the final form was expressive of the behaviour of the constituent structural materials.

In the IBM pilot head office building, the relationship between structure and architecture is less direct than in the other buildings described in this section and is perhaps significantly different to warrant a different terminology, namely *structure accepted*. In this kind of relationship, a form is adopted which is sensible structurally but the architectural interest is not closely related to structural function. This is a relationship between structure and architecture which is commonly found in contemporary architecture and innumerable other examples could be cited. It has, in fact, been the dominant relationship between structure and architecture since the time of the Italian Renaissance (see Section 7.3).

7.2.5 Structure ignored in the form-making process and not forming part of the aesthetic programme

Since the development of the structural technologies of steel and reinforced concrete it has been possible to design buildings, at least to a preliminary stage of the process, without considering how they will be supported or constructed. This is possible because the strength properties of steel and reinforced concrete are such that practically any form can be built, provided that it is not too large and that finance is not a limiting consideration. This freedom represents a significant and often unacknowledged contribution which structural technology has made to architecture, liberating architects from the constraints imposed by the need to support buildings with masonry and timber.

For most of the period following the introduction of steel and reinforced concrete into building in the late nineteenth century, the dominant architecture in the industrialised world was that of International Modernism. Most of the architects of this movement subscribed to

the doctrine of rationalism and held the view that buildings should be tectonic, i.e. they believed that the visual vocabulary should emerge from, or at least be directly related to, the structural armature of the building, which should be determined by rational means. The consequence of this was that the forms of most buildings were relatively straightforward from a structural point of view – based on the geometry of the post-and-beam framework.

An additional factor which favoured the use of simple forms was that the design and construction of very complex forms was laborious and costly, thus inhibiting the full exploitation of the potential offered by these new materials. There were of course exceptions. Erich Mendelsohn's Einstein Tower in Potsdam (see Fig. iii), Gerrit Rietveld's Schroeder House in Utrecht and Le Corbusier's chapel at Ronchamp (Fig. 7.40) were successfully realised despite having complex forms unrelated to structural function. Their relatively small scale meant that it was not difficult in each case to produce a structural armature which would support the form, rather in the manner of the armature of a sculpture.

Fig. 7.40 Notre-Dame-du-Haut, Ronchamp, France, 1954; Le Corbusier, architect. Structural considerations have played very little part in the determination of the form of this building. Its small scale together with the excellent structural properties of reinforced concrete, which was used for the roof, meant that it could be constructed without difficulty. (Photo: P. Macdonald)

The introduction of the computer in the late twentieth century, firstly as a tool for structural analysis and subsequently as a design aid, which allowed very complex forms to be described and cutting and fabricating processes to be controlled, gave architects almost unlimited freedom in the matter of form. This was a major factor in the introduction of the very complex geometries which appeared in architecture towards the end of the twentieth century. A good example is Frank Gehry's highly complex and spectacular Guggenheim Museum in Bilbao, Spain.

Wolf Prix, of Coop Himmelblau, was another late-twentieth-century architects who fully exploited this freedom:

'... we want to keep the design moment
free of all material constraints ...'[25]
'In the initial stages structural planning is
never an immediate priority ...'[26]

Great ingenuity was often required of the engineers who devised the structural solutions for buildings whose forms had been devised in a purely sculptural way. That of the chapel at Ronchamp is remarkable due to the great simplicity of the structure which supports the free-form roof. The walls of the building are of self-supporting stone masonry rendered white. There is a gap between the tops of these and the underside of the roof so as to admit a small amount of light into the interior in a gesture which is architecturally significant. The walls do not therefore carry the weight of the roof.

The upwardly curving, oversailing roof is formed by a thin shell of reinforced concrete which conceals an integral and conventional post-and-beam reinforced concrete framework. Reinforced concrete columns of small cross-section are embedded in the masonry walls in a regular grid, and carry beams which span across the building. These provide support from above for the roof shell, which sweeps up at the edges of the building to conceal them. Thus, although the overall form of the building bears no relation to the manner in which it functions structurally, a satisfactory and relatively simple structure was accommodated within it.

In more recent times a similar approach to that adopted by Le Corbusier at Ronchamp, at least so far as the relationship of structure to architecture is concerned, is to be found in the works of the architects of the Deconstruction school. The structural organisation of buildings such as the rooftop office in Vienna by Coop Himmelblau (see Fig. 1.11) or the Vitra Design Museum in Basel by Frank Gehry (Fig. 7.41) were relatively straightforward. The same may be said of Daniel Libeskind's Jewish Museum in Berlin (Fig. 7.42). More complex arrangements were required to realise the complicated geometries of Libeskind's extension to the Victoria and Albert Museum in London (Figs 7.43 and 7.44) and the new Imperial War Museum in Manchester.

Two important considerations must be taken into account when form is devised without recourse to structural requirements. Firstly, because the form will almost certainly be non-form-active, bending-type internal force will have to be resisted. Secondly, the magnitudes of the internal forces which are generated are likely to be high in relation to the load carried. The implications of both of these considerations are that structural material will be inefficiently used and that the element sizes required to produce adequate strength will be high. This is a scenario which can result in structures which are clumsy and ungainly.

A scale effect also operates because the strength of structural material remains constant even though the size of the structure increases. As was discussed in Chapter 6, all structural forms, whatever their shape, tend to become less efficient as spans increase. The maximum span for a given form occurs when the strength of the material is fully occupied, supporting the self-weight of the structure. If

25 Quotations from *On the Edge*, the contribution of Wolf Prix of Coop Himmelblau to Noever, P. (Ed.), *Architecture in Transition: Between Deconstruction and New Modernism*, Prestel-Verlag, Munich, 1991.

26 *Ibid*.

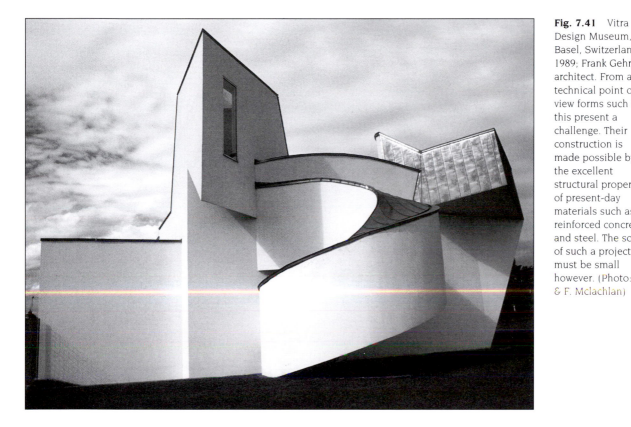

Fig. 7.41 Vitra Design Museum, Basel, Switzerland, 1989; Frank Gehry, architect. From a technical point of view forms such as this present a challenge. Their construction is made possible by the excellent structural properties of present-day materials such as reinforced concrete and steel. The scale of such a project must be small however. (Photo: E. & F. Mclachlan)

Fig. 7.42 Jewish Museum, Berlin, 1999; Daniel Libeskind Architekturburo, architects. The use of a reinforced concrete structural framework has allowed both a highly sculptured overall form to be created and a high degree of freedom to be achieved in the treatment of the non-structural cladding of the exterior.

Fig. 7.43 Design for an extension to the Victoria and Albert Museum, London, UK, 1995–; Daniel Libeskind Architekturburo, architects; Ove Arup & Partners, structural engineers. Structural considerations had little influence on the original design for this building.

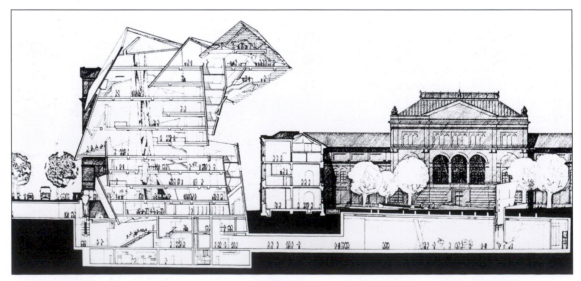

Fig. 7.44 Design for an extension to the Victoria and Albert Museum, London, UK, 1995–; Daniel Libeskind Architekturburo, architects; Ove Arup & Partners, structural engineers. The cross-section reveals that the structure is a fairly conventional post-and-beam framework. The relatively small scale of the project, the excellent properties of modern structural materials and the judicious use of structural continuity allowed this complex form to be realised.

the form adopted is fundamentally inefficient, because it has been designed without reference to structural requirements, the maximum possible span may be quite small.

The neglect of structural issues in the determination of the form of a building can therefore be problematic if a large span is involved. The small scale of the buildings already mentioned meant that the internal forces were not so large that they could not be resisted without the use of excessively large cross-sections. Eero Saarinen's terminal for TWA at Idlewild (now Kennedy) Airport, New York (Fig. 7.45) paid similar disregard to structural logic. Although the roof of this building was a reinforced concrete shell it did not have a form-active shape. The form was determined from visual rather than from structural considerations and, because it was larger than Ronchamp, difficulties occurred with the structure. These were overcome by modifying the original design to strengthen the shell in the locations of highest internal force.

Jorn Utzon's Sydney Opera House is another example of this type of building (Fig. 7.46). In this case, the scale was such that it was impossible to overcome the consequences of the complete disregard of structural and constructional concerns in the determination of the form. In the resulting saga, in which the form of the building had to be radically altered for constructional reasons, the architect resigned and the client was faced with a protracted construction period and with costs which were an order of magnitude greater than had originally been envisaged. Amid great political controversy, the building was nevertheless completed and has become a distinctive image which is synonymous with Sydney, if not with Australia, rather as the Eiffel Tower, Big Ben or the Statue of Liberty have come to represent other famous cities and their respective countries. Although the expertise of Ove Arup and Partners in solving the structural and constructional problems brought about by Utzon's inspired, if technically flawed, original design are undisputed, the question of whether the final form of the Sydney Opera House is good

Fig. 7.45 TWA Terminal, Idlewild (now Kennedy) Airport, New York, USA, 1962; Eero Saarinen, architect; Amman and Whitney, structural engineers. The form here was far from ideal structurally and strengthening ribs of great thickness were required at locations of high internal force. The structure was therefore inefficient but construction was possible due to the relatively modest spans involved. (Photo: R. J. Mainstone)

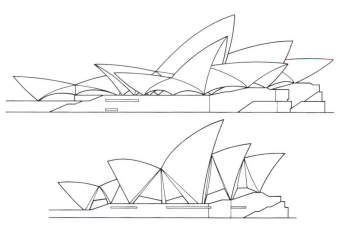

Fig. 7.46 Opera House, Sydney, Australia, 1957–65; Jorn Utzon, architect; Ove Arup & Partners, structural engineers. The upper drawing here shows the original competition-winning proposal for the building which proved impossible to build. The final scheme, though technically ingenious, is considered by many to be much less satisfactory visually. The significant difference between this and the buildings in Figs 7.41 to 7.45 is one of scale.

architecture remains open. This building may serve as a warning to architects who choose to disregard the inconveniences of structural requirements when determining form. The consequence may be that the final form will be different from their original vision in ways which they may be unable to control. The ignoring of structural logic in the creation of form is indeed possible but only in the context of short spans. The success of the recent buildings by Coop Himmelblau, Gehry and Libeskind has depended on this situation.

In all of the buildings considered in this section the structure is present in order to do its mundane job of supporting the building envelope. In this kind of architecture structural engineers act as facilitators – the people who make the building stand up. It should not be thought, however, that the world of structures has played no part in the evolution of the free-form architecture which became fashionable in the late twentieth century. It was the structural techniques which were developed in the twentieth century which made such an architecture possible, and which gave architects the freedom to exploit geometries which in previous centuries would have been impossible to realise.

7.2.6 Conclusion

This section has reviewed the interaction between structure and architecture and has shown that this can operate in a variety of ways. It is hoped that the several categories which have been identified for this relationship, however artificial they may be, nevertheless contribute to the understanding of the processes and interactions which constitute architectural design.

Six broad categories were identified and these may be considered to be grouped in different ways – something which sheds further light on the design process. One grouping would be to subdivide the various types of relationship into two broad categories – *structure exposed* and *structure hidden from view*. There are three sub-categories of the *structure exposed* relationship: *ornamentation of structure*, *structure as ornament* and *structure as architecture*. *Structure hidden* also contains two sub-categories: *structure as form generator/ structure accepted* and *structure ignored*.

The original six categories may alternatively be considered as grouped into two other overarching categories namely *structure respected*, in which forms are adopted which perform well when judged by technical criteria, and *structure disrespected*, in which little account is taken of structural requirements when the form is determined. The first of these would include *ornamentation of structure, structure as architecture, structure as form generator* and *structure accepted*. The second would include *structure as ornament* and *structure ignored*.

This second way of regarding the various possible relationships between structure and architecture focuses attention on the types of collaboration which can exist between architects and engineers, a fascinating aspect of the history of architecture. If structure is to be respected, engineers and architects must collaborate in a positive way over the design of a building. The engineer is then a member of the team of designers which evolves the form of the building. Where the relationships fall into the category of *structure disrespected* the engineer can be simply a technician – the person who works out how to build a form which has been determined by someone else.

7.3 The relationship between architects and engineers

Collaboration has always been required between architects and those who have the technical expertise to realise buildings. The nature of the relationship has taken many forms, and the form in play at any time has always influenced the nature of the interface between structure and architecture.

In Greek and Roman antiquity, the relationship between the equivalents of architects and engineers must have been very close in order to achieve the creation of buildings in which the requirements of structure and architecture were reconciled in a very positive way. In this period the architect and engineer would, in many cases, have been the same individual – the master builder. This

Fig. 7.47 Villa Emo, Fanzolo, Italy, 1564; Andrea Palladio, architect. Structural requirements exerted a strong influence on the form of this masonry and timber building but the architectural interest lay elsewhere.

(a)

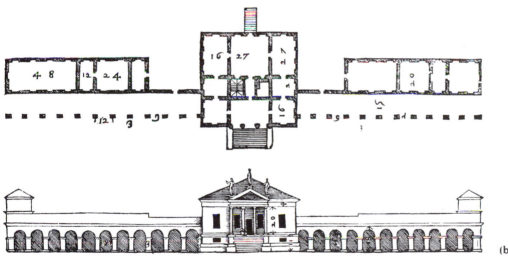

(b)

methodology brought into being some of the greatest buildings of the European Classical tradition, always in the context of *structure respected*. *Ornamentation of structure* produced the Greek temples (Fig. 7.1) and the Roman triumphal arches. *Structure as form generator* was the relationship that existed in the creation of the great interiors of Imperial Rome such as the Pantheon (Fig. 7.30) and the Basilica of Constantine (Fig. 7.31). In each case the relationship between structure and architecture was positive; the architecture was born out of a need to satisfy structural requirements. It meant that those responsible for the technical make-up of buildings also

played a significant role in determining their architectural qualities and interest.

This type of relationship between the equivalents of architects and engineers was maintained during the medieval period in which the Gothic buildings, which were a version of *ornamentation of structure*, were produced but it almost disappeared at the time of the Italian Renaissance.

Andrea Palladio, for example, who began his working life as a stone mason and who was entirely confident in the technology at his disposal, designed buildings which were practical and sensible from a structural viewpoint (Fig. 7.47). They belonged in the

115

Fig. 7.48 St Paul's Cathedral, London, UK, 17th century; Sir Christopher Wren, architect. In treatment of both the dome and the exterior wall the structural arrangement is not reflected in the visual programme.

category *structure accepted* rather than *structure as form generator*, however, because the architectural interest of his work lay in the idea of the building as a microcosm and his use of harmonic proportion, hierarchical arrangements of space and innovative uses of classical forms of ornamentation. The means by which the buildings were constructed were of little relevance to this agenda.

In Western architecture most of the buildings from the Italian Renaissance to the Modern period fall into this category. It is significant that throughout this period the principal structural materials were masonry and timber. These are problematic structurally in various ways[27] and forced architects to adopt

structural forms which were sensible from a structural point of view. The requirements of structure had therefore to be respected but, in the majority of buildings, the architectural interest lay elsewhere. This meant that structural considerations fell out of any discussion of architecture.

Two aspects of post-medieval architecture contributed to this. Firstly, a subtle change occurred in the nature of the relationship between structure and architecture because the structural armatures of buildings were increasingly concealed behind forms of ornamentation which were not directly related to structural function. The villa illustrated in Fig. 7.47 is an example by Palladio. His design for the Palazzo Valmarana in Vicenza (Fig. 7.2) is another. The Corinthian Order pilasters which were incorporated into the façade of this building formed the thin outer skin of a solid wall. The wall was the structural element and

---

27 See Macdonald, A. J., *Structural Design for Architecture*, Architectural Press, Oxford, 1997, Chapters 5 and 6 for a discussion of these issues.

Fig. 7.49 St Paul's Cathedral, London, UK, 17th century, Sir Christopher Wren, architect. The cross-section of the building reveals that the structural arrangement is conventional with a high central nave and flying buttresses carrying the side thrusts created by the masonry vault. The structural action is concealed behind the external wall, the upper half of which is a non-structural screen.

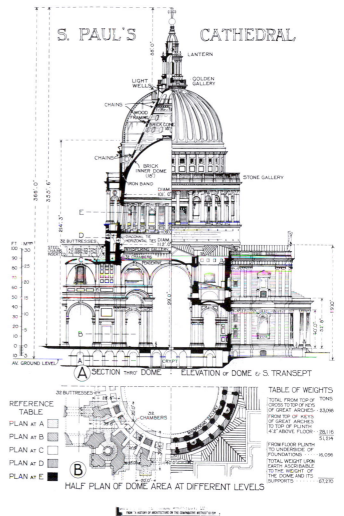

Fig. 7.50 St Paul's Cathedral, London, UK, 17th century; Sir Christopher Wren, architect. The dome is in three parts. The innermost part is a self-supporting masonry hemisphere. The outer skin is mounted on a timber framework supported by a cone of structural brickwork.

the pilasters had a symbolic rather than a structural role. The reduction of elements with structural origins to components in a visual vocabulary, which was typical of the architecture of the period, caused the structural and aesthetic agendas to drift apart. This in turn had a profound effect on the type of relationship which developed between architects and those who were responsible for the technical aspects of the design of a building.

The second change that occurred from the Italian Renaissance onwards was that most buildings were structurally unambitious. A technology of masonry walls and timber floor and roof structures existed whose capabilities were well understood and which presented little challenge to builders. There were obvious exceptions, Brunelleschi's dome in Florence being an excellent example (Fig. 7.13), but in the majority of buildings there was no sense of excitement in relation to the structural make-up. The forms adopted were sensible from a structural point of view, but there were no further structural ambitions. Even with large buildings such as St Paul's Cathedral in London (Figs 7.48 to 7.50) in which serious structural challenges had to be met, the structure made no obvious contribution to the architecture.

For example, the stone external walls of this building form a wallpaper-like screen, wrapped around the core of the building, which bears little relation to its structural make-up. The cross-section of the building is similar to that of a medieval Gothic church and consists of a high vaulted central nave flanked by lower aisles and with flying buttresses providing lateral support for the vault (Fig. 7.49). None of this is visible, or suggested, on the exterior.

The uncoupling of the structural from the visual agenda at St Paul's also occurred in the design of the dome, where Wren did not require that the interior and exterior profiles bear any relation to each other. The dome was constructed in three layers (Fig. 7.50). The part which is visible in the interior is a self-supporting structure – a semi-form-active

hemisphere in masonry. On the exterior, the profile of the dome is completely disconnected from the way in which it operates structurally. The structure is a cone of brickwork which is entirely hidden from view and which supports directly the stone cupola at the apex of the dome. The external profile of the dome is a lightweight skin supported on a timber formwork built out from the structural core. The brick cone conforms to the form-active shape for the principal load which it carries – that of the weight of the cupola – but its shape bears no relation to the form of the dome which is seen on either the interior or the exterior of the building. The architecture of the exterior of St Paul's, including that of the external wall and of the dome, is therefore unrelated visually to the structure which supports it.

Fig. 7.51 Train shed, St Pancras Station, London, UK, 1865; W. H. Barlow and R. M. Ordish, engineers. The architectural qualities of the large iron-and-glass interiors of the nineteenth century went largely unrecognised at the time.

The distance between the architectural and structural agendas was perhaps generally at its greatest towards the end of the nineteenth century and is exemplified by buildings such as St Pancras Station in London (1865). Here, one of the largest iron and glass vaults of the century, by W. H. Barlow and R. M. Ordish (Fig. 7.51), a spectacular example of what could be achieved with the new technology of structural iron, was concealed behind the bulk of Gilbert Scott's Midland Hotel in the High Victorian Gothic style (Fig. 7.52). The two parts of the building were each fine examples of their type, but they inhabited different worlds. The architectural qualities of the train shed went unrecognised: it was considered as simply a vulgar product of industry, necessary but not beautiful, and the citizens of London were protected from the sight of it by a fine essay in Ruskinian northern-Italian Gothic.

The visual disconnection of architecture from structure which is seen at St Paul's

Fig. 7.52 Midland Hotel, at St Pancras Station, London, UK, 1871; G. Gilbert Scott, architect. The form of the train shed did not influence the architectural agenda at St Pancras.

Cathedral and St Pancras Station illustrates well the approach which was adopted by Western architects from the Italian Renaissance onwards. Architects were still interested in structure, but only as a means of realising built form which was generated from ideas which were remote from technical considerations. This approach to architecture was made easier following the development of the structural technologies of steel and reinforced concrete in the late nineteenth century and it was used in much of the Modern architecture of the twentieth century. Steel and reinforced concrete had much better structural properties than timber or masonry and released architects from the need to pay attention to structural requirements, at least in cases where the limits of what was technically feasible were not being approached. This made possible, in the twentieth century, a new kind of relationship between structure and architecture – *structure ignored*.

A consequence of the distancing of the aesthetic from the technical agenda, the making of a distinction between architecture and building, was that architects no longer evolved the forms of buildings in a truly collaborative partnership with those who were responsible for the technical aspects of design. The latter became technicians, responsible for ensuring that the technical performance of a building would be satisfactory but not contributing creatively to its form or appearance.

Several of the prominent early Modern architects were, however, interested in tectonics, the architectural expression of the fundamental elements of buildings that are responsible for holding them up. This caused more collaborative relationships between architects and engineers to develop. The *status quo* was nevertheless maintained concerning the relationships between architects and engineers, and the design of a building was still very much dominated by the architect as the leader of the group of professionals who collaborated over its production. Modernism espoused rationalism but carried with it much of the baggage of nineteenth-century

Romanticism. One particularly strong aspect of this situation was the idea of the architect as a heroic figure – in the parlance of architectural criticism, the 'Modern Master'. Thus, although architecture became ever more dependent upon new structural technologies in the twentieth century and therefore upon the skill and expertise of engineers, most architects continued to behave, as they had done since the Italian Renaissance, as the masters of the design process and to treat the other designers involved as mere technicians. This view was endorsed by most of the critics and historians of Modernism who paid little regard to the technology which underpinned the Modern aesthetic and gave scant acknowledgement to the engineers who developed it. The names of the engineers of the classic buildings of early Modernism by architects such as Walter Gropius, Ludwig Mies van der Rohe and Le Corbusier are rarely mentioned.

The subservient position of engineers in relation to the conceptual stages of architectural design was maintained through the Modern period and has continued into the present day, where it may be observed to be still operating in some of the most prestigious architectural projects. The extremely complex forms devised by architects such as Frank Gehry (Fig. 7.41), Zaha Hadid or Daniel Libeskind (Figs 7.43 and 7.44), for example, provide serious challenges to engineers, but the engineers are not involved in the initial determination of the form.

A new type of relationship between architects and engineers, in which very positive collaborations occurred with engineers influencing the design of buildings from the very earliest stages, did, however, develop in the twentieth century. The catalyst which made this possible was the re-introduction of tectonics into the architectural discourse. This drew attention to the visual qualities of the emerging structural technologies of ferrous metal and reinforced concrete. It resulted in the re-examination, from an architectural point of view, of much nineteenth-century building that had escaped the notice of a contemporary architectural culture which had been preoccupied with revivals and 'battles of styles'. Buildings such as the Crystal Palace and the long-span train sheds of the mid-nineteenth century were seen by some early Modernists to have interesting architectural qualities. Buildings created by twentieth-century equivalents of the railway engineers were also considered to be worthy of attention and were given space in the architectural media. Thus, aircraft hangars (surely the twentieth-century equivalent of the train shed) by engineers such as Eugène Freyssinet (Fig. 7.14) and Pier Luigi Nervi, were praised for their architectural qualities and this led to the concept of the architect/engineer. The emergence of the architect/engineers (Eduardo Torroja, Ricardo Morandi, Owen Williams, and, in more recent times, Félix Candela and Santiago Calatrava are further examples) was a significant event in twentieth-century architecture. All these individuals have enjoyed the same kind of status as the leading architects of their day.

The gap which had long existed between architects and engineers was not closed by these engineers operating *as* architects rather than *with* architects. They have continued an established way of working in which the architect behaved very much as the leader of the design team, with structural engineers and other technical specialists playing a secondary role and making little direct and positive contribution to the visual aspects of a design. It must be said that many engineers are very happy to work in this way and to leave the architectural aspects of a design to architects and, in appropriate circumstances, a good building may be the result.

In the late twentieth century, however, a different way of working also became established: certain groups of architects and engineers evolved highly collaborative relationships, working in design teams of architects, structural engineers, services engineers and quantity surveyors, in which buildings were evolved through a discursive process. In this very close type of working relationship, all of the professionals involved contributed to the evolution of a design which

emerged as a truly joint effort. It was this method of working which made possible the style known as High Tech in which structure and services components formed major aspects of the visual vocabulary of buildings.

The collaborations between architects, such as Norman Foster, Nicholas Grimshaw, Michael Hopkins and Richard Rogers with engineers such as Ted Happold, Tony Hunt and Peter Rice, have been particularly effective. The working methodology involved regular discursive meetings of the design teams in which all aspects of the design were discussed. The closeness of the collaborations was such that often, in retrospect, it was not possible to attribute many aspects of the final design to any particular individual[28].

It was in this spirit that the best twentieth-century examples of *ornamentation of structure* were produced (for example Reliance Controls (Fig. 7.4) and the Waterloo Terminal (Fig. 7.17)). The *genre* has continued into the twenty-first century with buildings such as the National Botanical Garden of Wales (Fig. 7.53) by Foster and Partners with Anthony Hunt Associates, and the Eden Project (Fig. 7.54) by Nicholas Grimshaw and Partners with Anthony Hunt Associates. In the latter cases (and this is also true of the earlier Waterloo building), a complexity of form has been accomplished which depends on the use of state-of-the-art techniques of computer-aided design. This type of architecture is a strand of Modernism which has retained its vitality through the period in the late twentieth century in which Postmodernism and Deconstruction have been fashionable (both of these being examples of styles in which much less creative relationships between structure and architecture have occurred[29]).

---

28 The design team methodology was especially favoured by Tony Hunt who carried out work with all of the leading High-Tech architects; see Macdonald A. J., *Anthony Hunt*, Thomas Telford, London, 2000.

29 Most Postmodern architecture falls into the category *structure accepted* while Deconstruction is mainly *structure ignored*.

Fig. 7.53 National Botanical Garden of Wales, 1999; Foster and Partners, architects, Anthony Hunt Associates, structural engineers. This innovative single-layer dome is a toroidal form executed in one-way-spanning tubular steel arches, of varying span, with orthogonal linking elements. Built form of this complexity in steelwork was not possible before the age of computer-aided design.

Fig. 7.54 The Eden Project, Cornwall, UK, 1999; Nicholas Grimshaw and Partners, architects; Anthony Hunt Associates, structural engineers. The complexity of form made possible by computer-aided design has brought into being a new generation of metal and glass structure.

The buildings in which the design-team methodology was used are generally regarded as belonging to the High-Tech school. The situation is, however, more complex, as more than one version of the relationship between structure and architecture is discernible in High Tech. Many of the High-Tech buildings have in fact been designed by traditional methods, with the architect attending principally to visual and stylistic issues and the engineer confining his or her actions mainly to the technical details of the structure. As has been shown, the design of buildings such as the Centre Pompidou was driven principally by visual agendas in which the architects must be regarded as having operated very much as the leaders of the design teams.

Where truly collaborative relationships have occurred, however, the kind of relationship between architectural and structural thinking which existed in antiquity and the Gothic period has been re-captured. In historic architecture, this existed in the form of the 'master builder'. The present-day design team, operating in a truly collaborative way and using state-of-the-art techniques of computer-aided design, as with Grimshaw and Hunt at Waterloo, is the modern equivalent of the master builder.

Three types of relationship between architects and engineers are currently in play.

In the overwhelming majority of Modern buildings, the relationship between architects and engineers which prevails is that which became established from the Italian Renaissance, namely a situation in which the architect determines the form of a building and sets the visual agenda, and the engineer acts principally as the technician who ensures that it performs adequately in a technical sense. This type of relationship between architects and engineers predominates in all of the sub-styles of Modernism including Postmodernism and Deconstruction.

A second type of relationship occurs where the architect and the engineer are the same person. Several prominent figures have operated in this way from the twentieth century onwards, including August Perret and Robert Maillart at the beginning of the century, Pier Luigi Nervi, Eduardo Torroja, Owen Williams and Félix Candela in the mid-twentieth century and Santiago Calatrava at the end of the twentieth century and in the present day. All of these architect/engineers have produced buildings in which the strategies involved have been those of *structure as architecture, structure as form generator* or *ornamentation of structure*. Their most memorable buildings have been long-span enclosures in the language of the form-active vault or tensile structure. The aesthetic agenda has been relatively simple – the appreciation of a building as a work of technology.

A third type of relationship between architects and engineers, that of a truly collaborative partnership, re-emerged towards the end of the twentieth century. This has involved engineers and architects co-operating fully over the design of a building in a way which had not occurred since their equivalents created the cathedrals of medieval Gothic. The best of the buildings of High Tech have been designed in this way.

In the present day, this third category of relationship is producing a new kind of architecture of great geometric complexity. The train shed at Waterloo Station by Hunt and Grimshaw (Fig. 7.17) is an early example. This building may appear to be simply a twentieth-century version of the nineteenth-century iron-and-glass railway station, with recent technical innovations such as weldable cast-steel joints. It may also appear to be High Tech. In fact, the steelwork possesses a level of complexity which could not have been accomplished before the age of computer-aided design and which is suggestive of the complexity of a living organism, one of the appropriate metaphors for the philosophies of the emerging organicist paradigm. Although, therefore, this building may be seen as a development of the High Tech style, it is significantly distinct to merit a different name, perhaps 'organi-tech'. The same could be said of the dome at the National Botanical Garden of Wales (Fig. 7.53) by Foster and Partners with Anthony Hunt Associates, and of the Eden Project (Fig. 7.54) by Nicholas Grimshaw and Partners, also with Anthony Hunt Associates.

The realisation of the complex organic or 'land-form'[30] shapes of these buildings gives appropriate visual expression to the sophistication of contemporary technology. They also provide 'intimations' in several senses of what might be involved in a 're-constructive' post-modern architectural practice[31] even while they remain linked to the Modernist agenda concerned with the celebration of technological progress.

30 This term was used by Charles Jencks in an article in Jencks, C. (Ed.), *New Science = New Architecture?*, Academy Editions, London, 1997, in which he discussed the non-linear architecture of architects such as Eisenman, Gehry, Koolhaus and Miralles.

31 See Gablik, S., *The Re-enchantment of Art*, Thames and Hudson, New York, 1991.

Selected bibliography

Addis, W., *The Art of the Structural Engineer*, Artemis, London, 1994.

Ambrose, J., *Building Structures*, John Wiley, New York, 1988.

Amery, C., *Architecture, Industry and Innovation: The Early Work of Nicholas Grimshaw and Partners*, Phaidon, London, 1995.

Baird, J. A. and Ozelton, E. C., *Timber Designer's Manual*, 2nd edition, Crosby Lockwood Staples, London, 1984.

Balcombe, G., *Mitchell's History of Building*, London, Batsford, 1985.

Benjamin, B. S., *Structures for Architects*, 2nd edition, Van Nostrand Reinhold, New York, 1984.

Benjamin, J. R., *Statically Indeterminate Structures*, McGraw-Hill, New York, 1959.

Billington, D. P., *Robert Maillart*, MIT Press, Cambridge, MA, 1989.

Billington, D. P., *The Tower and the Bridge*, Basic Books, New York, 1983.

Blanc, A., McEvoy, M. and Plank, R., *Architecture and Construction in Steel*, E. & F. N. Spon, London, 1993.

Blaser, W. (Ed.), *Santiago Calatrava – Engineering Architecture*, Borkhauser Verlag, Basel, 1989.

Boaga, G. and Boni, B., *The Concrete Architecture of Riccardo Morandi*, Tiranti, London, 1965.

Breyer, D. E. and Ark, J. A., *Design of Wood Structures*, McGraw-Hill, New York, 1980.

Broadbent, G., *Deconstruction: A Student Guide*, Academy, London, 1991.

Brookes, A. and Grech, C., *Connections: Studies in Building Assembly*, Butterworth-Heinemann, Oxford, 1992.

Burchell, J. and Sunter, F. W., *Design and Build in Timber Frame*, Longman, London, 1987.

Ching, F. D. K., *Building Construction Illustrated*, Van Nostrand Reinhold, New York, 1975.

Coates, R. C., Coutie, M. G. and Kong, F. K., *Structural Analysis*, 3rd edition, Van Nostrand Reinhold, Wokingham, 1988.

Conrads, U. (Ed.), *Programmes and Manifestos on Twentieth Century Architecture*, Lund Humphries, London, 1970.

Corbusier, Le, *Five Points Towards a New Architecture*, Paris, 1926.

Corbusier, Le, *Towards a New Architecture*, Architectural Press, London, 1927.

Cowan, H. J., *Architectural Structures*, Elsevier, New York, 1971.

Cowan, H. J. and Wilson, F., *Structural Systems*, Van Nostrand Reinhold, New York, 1981.

Cox, H. L., *The Design of Structures of Least Weight*, Pergamon, London, 1965.

Curtis, W. J. R., *Modern Architecture Since 1900*, Phaidon, London, 1982.

Davies, C., *High Tech Architecture*, Thames & Hudson, London, 1988.

De Compoli, G., *Statics of Structural Components*, John Wiley, New York, 1983.

Denyer, S., *African Traditional Architecture*, Heinemann, London, 1978.

Dowling, P. J., Knowles, P. and Owens, G. W., *Structural Steel Design*, Butterworths, London, 1988.

Drew, P., *Frei Otto*, Granada Publishing, London, 1976.

Elliott, C. D., *Technics and Architecture: The Development of Materials and Systems for Buildings*, MIT Press, London, 1992.

Engel, H., *Structure Systems*, Deutsche Verlags-Anstalt, Stuttgart, 1967.

Engel, H., *Structural Principles*, Prentice-Hall, Englewood Cliffs, NJ, 1984.

Everett, A., *Materials*, Mitchell's Building Series, Batsford, London, 1986.

Fraser, D. J., *Conceptual Designs and Preliminary Analysis of Structures*, Pitman Marshfield, MA, 1981.

Gablik, S., *Has Modernism Failed?*, Thames & Hudson, London, 1984.

Gablik, S., *The Re-enchantment of Art*, Thames and Hudson, New York, 1991.

Gheorghiu, A. and Dragomit, V., *The Geometry of Structural Forms*, Applied Science Publishers, London, 1978.

Glancey, J., *New British Architecture*, Thames & Hudson, London, 1990.

Gordon, J. E., *Structures*, Pelican, London, 1978.

Gordon, J. E., *The New Science of Strong Materials*, Pelican, London, 1968.

Gorst, T., *The Buildings Around Us*, E. & F. N. Spon, London, 1995.

Gössel, P. and Leuthäuser, G., *Architecture in the Twentieth Century*, Benedikt Taschen, Cologne, 1991.
Groak, S., *The Idea of Building*, E. & F. N. Spon, London, 1992.

Hammond, R., *The Forth Bridge and its Builders*, Eyre & Spottiswood, London, 1964.

Hart, F., Henn, W. and Sontag, H., *Multi Storey Buildings in Steel*, Crosby Lockwood Staples, London, 1976.

Heinle, E. and Leonhardt, F., *Towers: A Historical Survey*, Butterworth Architecture, London, 1988.

Herzog, T., *Pneumatic Structures*, Crosby Lockwood Staples, London, 1976.

Holgate, A., *The Art in Structural Design*, Clarendon Press, Oxford, 1986.

Holgate, A., *Aesthetics of Built Form*, Oxford University Press, Oxford, 1992.

Horvath, K. A., *The Selection of Load-bearing Structures for Buildings*, Elsevier, London, 1986.

Howard, H. S., *Structure: An Architect's Approach*, McGraw-Hill, New York, 1966.

Hunt, A., *Tony Hunt's Structures Notebook*, Architectural Press, Oxford, 1997.

Hunt, A., *Tony Hunt's Sketchbook*, Architectural Press, Oxford, 1999.

Huxtable, A. L., *The Tall Building Reconsidered: The Search for a Skyscraper Style*, Pantheon Books, New York, 1984.

Jan van Pelt, R. and Westfall, C., *Architectural Principles in the Age of Historicism*, Yale University Press, New Haven, 1991.

Jencks, C., *The Language of Post-modern Architecture*, 3rd edition, Academy, London, 1981.

Jencks, C., *Modern Movements in Architecture*, Penguin Books, Harmondsworth, 1985.

Joedicke, J., *Shell Architecture*, Karl Kramer Verlag, Stuttgart, 1963.

Kong, F. K. and Evans, R. H., *Reinforced and Prestressed Concrete*, 2nd edition, Van Nostrand Reinhold, New York, 1981.

Lambot, I. (Ed.), *Norman Foster: Foster Associates: Buildings and Projects*, Vols 1–4, Watermark, Hong Kong, 1989–90.

Lin, T. Y. and Stotesbury, S. D., *Structural Concepts and Systems for Architects and Engineers*, John Wiley, New York, 1981.

Macdonald, A. J., *Wind Loading on Buildings*, Applied Science Publishers, London, 1975.

Macdonald, A. J., *Structural Design for Architecture*, Architectural Press, Oxford, 1997.

Macdonald, A. J. and Boyd Whyte, I., *The Forth Bridge*, Axel Menges, Stuttgart, 1997.

Macdonald, A. J., *Anthony Hunt*, Thomas Telford, London, 2000.

Mainstone, R., *Developments in Structural Form*, Allen Lane, Harmondsworth, 1975.

Mainstone, R., 'Brunelleschi's Dome', *The Architectural Review*, CLXII (967) 156–166, Sept. 1977.

Majid, K. I., *Optimum Design of Structures*, Newnes-Butterworths, London, 1974.

Makowski, Z. S., *Steel Space Structures*, Michael Joseph, London, 1965.

Marder, T. (Ed.), *The Critical Edge: Controversy in Recent American Architecture*, MIT Press, Cambridge, MA, 1985.

Mark, R., *Light, Wind and Structure*, MIT Press, Cambridge, MA, 1990.

Mettem, C. J., *Structural Timber Design and Technology*, Longman, London, 1986.

Morgan, W., *The Elements of Structure*, 2nd edition (revised I. G. Buckle), Longman, London, 1978.

Morgan, W. and Williams, D. T., *Structural Mechanics*, 5th edition (revised F. Durka), Longman, London, 1996.

Morris, A., *Precast Concrete in Architecture*, George Godwin, London, 1978.

Nervi, P. L., *Structures*, McGraw-Hill, New York, 1956.

Nervi, P. L., *Aesthetics and Technology in Building*, Harvard University Press, Cambridge, MA, 1956.

Neville, A. R., *Properties of Concrete*, 3rd edition, Longman, London, 1986.

Noever, P. (Ed.), *Architecture in Transition: Between Deconstruction and New Modernism*, Prestel-Verlag, Munich, 1991.

Orton, A., *The Way We Build Now*, E. & F. N. Spon, London, 1988.

Otto, F., *Tensile Structures*, MIT Press, Cambridge, MA, 1973.

Papadakis, E., *Engineering and Architecture*, Architectural Design Profile No. 70, Academy, London, 1987.

Pawley, M., *Theory and Design in the Second Machine Age*, Basil Blackwell, Oxford, 1990.

Piano, R., *Projects and Buildings 1964–1983*, Architectural Press, London, 1984.

Rice, P., *An Engineer Imagines*, Ellipsis, London, 1994.

Robbin, T., *Engineering a New Architecture*, Yale University Press, New Haven, 1996.

Salvadori, M., *Why Buildings Stand Up*, W. W. Norton, London, 1980.

Schodek, D. L., *Structures*, Prentice-Hall, Englewood Cliffs, NJ, 1980.

Schueller, W., *High-rise Building Structures*, John Wiley, London, 1977.

Scully, V., *The Earth, the Temple and the Gods*, Yale University Press, New Haven, 1979.

Siegel, K., *Structure and Form in Modern Architecture*, Reinhold, New York, 1962.

Strike, J., *Construction Into Design*, Butterworth Architecture, Oxford, 1991.

Sunley, J. and Bedding, B. (Ed.), *Timber in Construction*, Batsford, London, 1985.

Szabo, J. and Koller, L., *Structural Design of Cable Suspended Roofs*, John Wiley, London, 1984.

Thornton, C., Tomasetti, R., Tuchman, J. and Joseph, L., *Exposed Structure in Building Design*, McGraw-Hill, New York, 1993.

Timoshenko, S. P. and Gere, J. H., *Mechanics of Materials* (SI Edition), Van Nostrand Reinhold, London, 1973.

Timoshenko, S. P. and Young, D. G., *Theory of Structures*, 2nd edition, McGraw-Hill, New York, 1965.

Torroja, E., *Philosophy of Structures*, University of California Press, Berkeley, 1958.

Torroja, E., *The Structures of Eduardo Torroja*, F. W. Dodge, New York, 1958.

Venturi, R., *Complexity and Contradiction in Architecture*, Museum of Modern Art, New York, 1966.

Walker, D. (Ed.), *The Great Engineers: The Art of British Engineers 1937–1987*, Academy Editions, London, 1987.

Watkin, D., *A History of Western Architecture*, Barrie & Jenkins, London, 1986.

Werner Rosenthal, H., *Structural Decisions*, Chapman and Hall, London, 1962.

West, H. H., *Analysis of Structures*, John Wiley, New York, 1980.

Wilkinson, C., *Supersheds: The Architecture of Long-span Large-volume Buildings*, Butterworth Architecture, Oxford, 1991.

Williams, D. T., Morgan, W. and Durka, F., *Structural Mechanics*, Pitman, London, 1980.

White, R. N., Gergely, P. and Sexsmith, R. G., *Structural Engineering*, Vol. 1, John Wiley, New York, 1976.

Windsor, A., *Peter Behrens*, Architectural Press, London, 1981.

Zalewski, W. and Allen, E., *Shaping Structures*, John Wiley, New York, 1998.

Zukowski, J. (Ed.), *Mies Reconsidered: His Career, Legacy, and Disciples*, Art Institute of Chicago, Chicago, 1986.

Appendix 1

Simple two-dimensional force systems and static equilibrium

A1.1 Introduction

Structures are devices for conducting forces from the points where they originate in buildings to foundations where they are ultimately resisted. They contain force systems which are in a state of static equilibrium. An appreciation of the concepts of force, equilibrium and the elementary properties of force systems is therefore fundamental to the understanding of structures.

A1.2 Force vectors and resultants

Force is a vector quantity which means that both its magnitude and its direction must be specified in order to describe it fully. It can be represented graphically by a line, called a vector, which is drawn parallel to its direction and whose length is proportional to its magnitude (Fig. A1.1). When two or more non-parallel forces act together, their combined effect is equivalent to that of a single force which is called the resultant of the original forces. The magnitude and direction of the resultant can be found graphically by vector addition in a 'triangle of forces' or a 'polygon of forces' (Fig. A1.2). In this type of addition the resultant is always represented, in both magnitude and direction, by the line which is required to close the 'triangle of forces' or 'polygon of forces'.

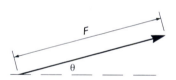

Fig. A1.1 Force is a vector quantity and can be represented by a line whose length is proportional to its direction and whose direction is parallel to its direction.

Fig. A1.2 Vector addition: the triangle and polygon of forces. (a) A body acted upon by two forces. (b) Vector addition produces a triangle of forces which yields the resultant. (c) The resultant has the same effect on the body as the original forces, and is therefore exactly equivalent to them. (d) A body acted upon by three forces. (e) Vector addition produces a polygon of forces which yields the resultant. (f) The resultant has the same effect on the body as the original group of forces.

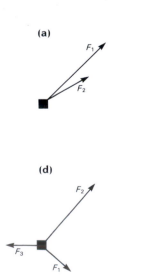

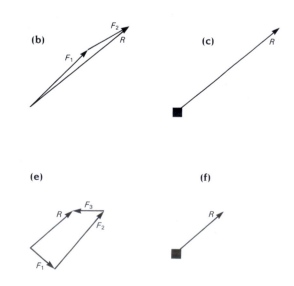

A1.3 Resolution of a force into components

Single forces can be subdivided into parts by reversing the process described above and considering them to be the resultant of two or more components (Fig. A1.3). The technique is called the resolution of the force into its components and it is useful because it allows force systems to be simplified into two sets of forces acting in orthogonal directions (i.e. two perpendicular directions). It also allows the addition of forces to be carried out algebraically rather than graphically. The resultant of the set of forces in Fig. A1.2, for example, is easily calculated if each of the forces is first resolved into its horizontal and vertical components (Fig. A1.4).

A1.4 Moments of forces

Forces exert a turning effect, called a moment, about points which are not on their line of action. The magnitude of this is equal to the product of the magnitude of the force and the perpendicular distance between its line of action and the point about which the turning effect occurs (Fig. A1.5).

A1.5 Static equilibrium and the equations of equilibrium

Structures are rigid bodies which are acted upon by external forces called loads. Their response to these depends on the characteristics of the force system. If the structure is acted upon by no force it may be

Fig. A1.3 Resolution of a force into components. (a) A single force. (b) A triangle of forces used to determine the vertical and horizontal components of the single force: $v = F \sin \theta$; $h = F \cos \theta$. (c) The vertical and horizontal components are exactly equivalent to the original force.

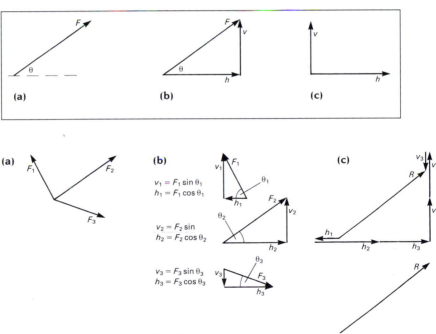

Fig. A1.4 Use of resolution of forces into components to determine the resultant of a set of forces. (a) Three concurrent forces. (b) Resolution of the forces into vertical and horizontal components. (c) Determination of the resultant by vector addition of the components.

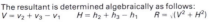

The resultant is determined algebraically as follows:
$$V = v_2 + v_3 - v_1 \qquad H = h_2 + h_3 - h_1 \qquad R = \sqrt{(V^2 + H^2)}$$

Fig. A1.5 The moment of a force about a point is simply a measure of the turning effect which it exerts about that point.

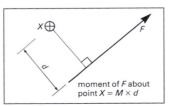

moment of F about point $X = M \times d$

regarded as being in a state of rest. If it is acted upon by a single force, or by a group of forces which has a resultant, it moves, (more precisely it accelerates) under their action (Fig. A1.6). The direction of the movement is the

Fig. A1.6   If a body is acted upon by a force it will accelerate along the line of action of the force. The magnitude of the acceleration depends on the relationship between the mass of the body and the magnitude of the force (Newton's Second Law of Motion).

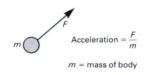

$$\text{Acceleration} = \frac{F}{m}$$

m = mass of body

same as that of the line of action of the single force or resultant and the rate of acceleration is dependent on the relationship between the mass of the structure and the magnitude of the force. If the structure is acted upon by a group of forces which has no resultant, that is a group of forces whose 'triangle of forces' or 'polygon of forces' is a closed figure, it may remain at rest and a state of static equilibrium is said to exist. This is the condition which is required of the force systems which act on real structures although, as will be seen below, the need for the force system to have no resultant

is a necessary but not a sufficient condition for equilibrium.

The loads which act on real structures rarely constitute an equilibrium set by themselves but equilibrium is established by reacting forces which act between the structures and their foundations. These reacting forces are in fact generated by the loads which tend to move the structure against the resisting effect of the supports. The relationship which exists between the loading forces which act on a structure and the reacting forces which these produce at its foundations is demonstrated here in a very simple example, which is illustrated in Fig. A1.7.

The example is concerned with the equilibrium or otherwise of a rigid body which is situated on a frictionless surface (a block of wood on a sheet of ice might be a practical example of this). In Fig. A1.7(a), a force (load) is applied to the body and, because the body is resting on a frictionless surface and no opposing force is possible, it moves in response to the force. In Fig. A1.7(b) the body encounters resistance in the form of an immovable object and as it is pushed against the object a reaction is generated whose

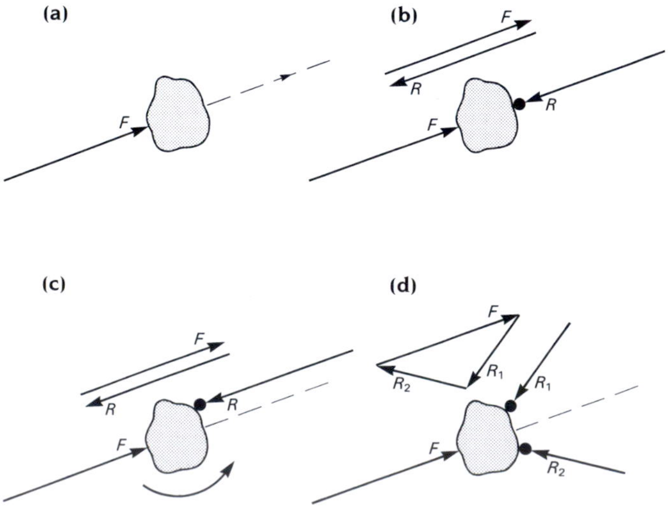

(a)

(b)

(c)

(d)

Fig. A1.7   Reacting forces are passive as they occur only as a result of other forces acting on objects. They are generated at locations where resistance is offered to the movement of the object. Equilibrium will occur only if the disposition of resistance points is such that the acting forces together with the reactions form a closed force polygon and exert no net turning effect on the object. The latter condition is satisfied if the sum of the moments of the forces about any point in their plane is zero. (a) A body accelerating under the action of a force. (b) Acceleration stopped and equilibrium established due to the presence of an immovable object on the line of action of the force. This generates a reaction which is equal and opposite to the acting force. Note the very simple 'polygon' of forces which the vector addition of the acting force and reaction produces. (c) Equilibrium is not established if the immovable object does not lie on the line of action of the force F, even though the polygon of forces produces no resultant. The latter means that translational motion will not occur but rotation is still possible. (d) A second immovable object restores equilibrium by producing a second reacting force. Note that the magnitude and direction of the original reaction are now different but the force polygon is still a closed figure with no resultant.

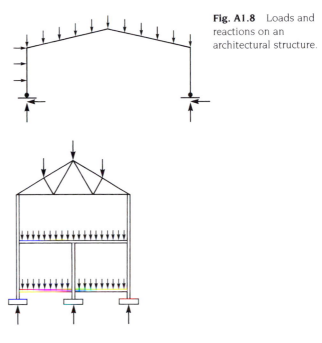

Fig. A1.8 Loads and reactions on an architectural structure.

magnitude increases as the pressure on the object increases until it is equal to that of the acting force. The reaction then balances the system and equilibrium is established.

In this case, because the object providing the resistance happened to lie on the line of action of the acting force, one source of resistance only was required to bring about equilibrium. If the object had not been in the line of action of the force as in Fig. A1.7(c), the reaction would together still have been developed, but the resultant and the reaction would have produced a turning effect which would have rotated the body. A second resisting object would then have been required to produce a second reaction to establish equilibrium (Fig. A1.7(d)). The existence of the new reaction would cause the magnitude of the original reaction to change, but the total force system would nevertheless continue to have no resultant, as can be seen from the force polygon, and would therefore be capable of reaching equilibrium. Because, in this case, the forces produce no net turning effect on the body, as well as no net force, a state of equilibrium would exist.

The simple system shown in Fig. A1.7 demonstrates a number of features which are possessed by the force systems which act on architectural structures (Fig. A1.8). The first is the function of the foundations of a structure which is to allow the development of such reacting forces as are necessary to balance the acting forces (i.e. the loads). Every structure must be supported by a foundation system which is capable of producing a sufficient number of reactions to balance the loading forces. The precise nature of the reactions which are developed depends on the characteristics of the loading system and on the types of supports which are provided; the reactions change if the loads acting on the structure change. If the structure is to be in equilibrium under all possible combinations of load, it must be supported by a foundation system which will allow the necessary reactions to be developed at the supports under all the load conditions.

The second feature which is demonstrated by the simple system in Fig. A1.7 is the set of conditions which must be satisfied by a force system if it is to be in a state of static equilibrium. In fact there are just two conditions; the force system must have no resultant in any direction and the forces must exert no net turning effect on the structure. The first of these is satisfied if the components of the forces balance (sum to zero) when they are resolved in any two directions and the second is satisfied if the sum of the moments of the forces about any point in their plane is zero. It is normal to check for the equilibrium of a force system algebraically by resolving the forces into two orthogonal directions (usually the vertical and horizontal directions) and the conditions for equilibrium in a two-dimensional system can therefore be summarised by the following three equations:

The sum of the vertical components of all of the forces $= 0$
$$\Sigma F_v = 0$$
The sum of the horizontal components of all of the forces $= 0$
$$\Sigma F_h = 0$$
The sum of the moments of all of the forces $= 0$
$$\Sigma M = 0$$

The two conditions for static equilibrium in a co-planar force system are the physical basis of all elementary structural calculations and the three equations of equilibrium which are derived from them are the fundamental relationships on which all of the elementary methods of structural analysis are based.

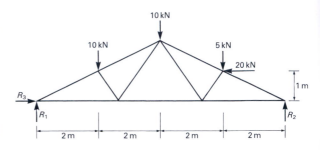

Fig. A1.9 Free-body-diagram of a roof truss.

A1.6 The 'free-body-diagram'

In the analysis of structures, the equations which summarise the conditions for equilibrium are used in conjunction with the concept of the 'free-body-diagram' to calculate the magnitudes of the forces which are present in structures. A 'free-body-diagram' is simply a diagram of a rigid object, the 'free body', on which all the forces which act on the body are marked. The 'free body' might be a whole structure or part of a structure and if, as it must be, it is in a state of equilibrium, the forces which act on it must satisfy the conditions for equilibrium. The equations of equilibrium can therefore be written for the forces which are present in the diagram and can be solved for any of the forces whose magnitudes are not known. For example, the three equations of equilibrium for the structure illustrated in Fig. A1.9 are:

Vertical equilibrium:
$$R_1 + R_2 = 10 + 10 + 5 \qquad (1)$$

Horizontal equilibrium:
$$R_3 - 20 = 0 \qquad (2)$$

Rotational equilibrium (taking moments about the left support):
$$10 \times 2 + 10 \times 4 + 5 \times 6 - 20 \times 1 - R_2 \times 8 = 0 \qquad (3)$$

The solutions to these are:

from equation (3), $R_2 = 8.75$ kN

from equation (2), $R_3 = 20$ kN

from equation (1), by substituting for R_2, $R_1 = 16.25$ kN

A1.7 The 'imaginary cut' technique

The 'imaginary cut' is a device for exposing internal forces as forces which are external to a free body which is part of the structure. This renders them accessible for analysis. In its simplest form this technique consists of imagining that the structural element is cut through at the point where the internal forces are to be determined and that one of the resulting two parts of it is removed. If this were done to a real structure the remaining part would, of course, collapse, but in this technique it is imagined that such forces as are necessary to maintain the remaining part in equilibrium in its original position, are applied to the face of the cut (Fig. A1.10). It is reasoned

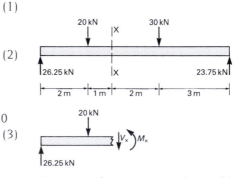

Fig. A1.10 The investigation of internal forces in a simple beam using the device of the 'imaginary cut'. The cut produces a free-body-diagram from which the nature of the internal forces at a single cross-section can be deduced. The internal forces at other cross-sections can be determined from similar diagrams produced by cuts made in appropriate places.

that these forces must be exactly equivalent to the internal forces which acted on that cross-section in the structure before the cut was made and the device of the imaginary cut therefore makes the internal forces accessible for equilibrium analysis by exposing them as forces which are external to a part of the structure. They then appear in the 'free-body-diagram' (see Section A1.6) of that part of the structure and can be calculated from the equations of equilibrium.

In the analysis of large structural arrangements the device of the 'imaginary cut' is used in several stages. The structure is first subdivided into individual elements (beams, columns, etc.) for which free-body-diagrams are drawn and the forces which pass between the elements are calculated from these. Each element is then further sub-divided by 'imaginary cuts' so that the internal forces at each cross-section can be determined. The procedure is summarised in Fig. 2.18.

Appendix 2

Stress and strain

A2.1 Introduction

Stress and strain are important concepts in the consideration of both strength and rigidity. They are inevitable and inseparable consequences of the action of load on a structural material. Stress may be thought of as the agency which resists load; strain is the measure of the deformation which occurs when stress is generated.

The stress in a structural element is the internal force divided by the area of the cross-section on which it acts. Stress is therefore internal force per unit area of cross-section; conversely internal force can be regarded as the accumulated effect of stress.

The strength of a material is measured in terms of the maximum stress which it can withstand – its failure stress. The strength of a structural element is the maximum internal force which it can withstand. This depends on both the strength of the constituent material and the size and shape of its cross-section. The ultimate strength of the element is reached when the stress level exceeds the failure stress of the material.

Several different types of stress can occur in a structural element depending on the direction of the load which is applied in relation to its principal dimension. If the load is coincident with the principal axis of the element it causes axial internal force and produces axial stress (Fig. A2.1). A load is called a bending-type load if its direction is perpendicular to the principal axis of the element (Fig. A2.2); this produces the internal forces of bending moment and shear force which cause a combination of bending stress and shear stress respectively to act on the cross-sectional planes of the element.

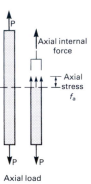

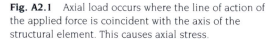

Fig. A2.1 Axial load occurs where the line of action of the applied force is coincident with the axis of the structural element. This causes axial stress.

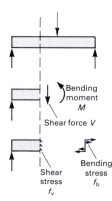

Fig. A2.2 Bending-type load occurs where the line of action of the applied force is perpendicular to the axis of the element. This causes bending and shear stress to occur on the cross-sectional planes.

The dimensional change which occurs to a specimen of material as a result of the application of load is expressed in terms of the dimensionless quantity strain. This is defined as the change in a specified dimension divided by the original value of that dimension. The

134

precise nature of strain depends on the type of stress with which it occurs. Axial stress produces axial strain, which occurs in a direction parallel to the principal dimension of the element and is defined as the ratio of the change in length which occurs, to the original length of the element (Fig. A2.3). Shear strain, to give another example, is defined in terms of the amount of angular distortion which occurs (Fig. A2.4).

Stress and strain are the quantities by which the mechanical behaviour of materials in response to load is judged. For a given load their magnitudes depend on the sizes of the structural elements concerned and they are therefore key quantities in the determination of element sizes. The size of cross-section must be such that the stress which results from the internal forces caused by the loads is less than the failure or yield stress of the material by an adequate margin. The rigidity is adequate if the deflection of the structure taken as a whole is not excessive.

A2.2 Calculation of axial stress

The axial stress in an element is uniformly distributed across the cross-section (Fig. A2.5) and is calculated from the following equation:

$$f = P/A$$

where: f = axial stress
P = axial thrust
A = area of cross-section.

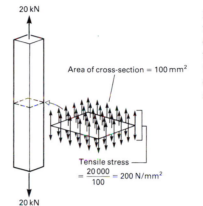

Fig. A2.5 Tensile stress on the cross-section of an element subjected to axial tension. The intensity of this is normally assumed to be constant across the cross-section.

Axial stress can be tensile or compressive. If the size of cross-section does not vary along the length of an element the magnitude of the axial stress is the same at all locations.

A2.3 Calculation of bending stress

Bending stress occurs in an element if the external loads cause bending moment to act on its cross-sections. The magnitude of the bending stress varies within each cross-section from maximum stresses in tension and compression in the extreme fibres on opposite sides of the cross-section, to a minimum stress in the centre (at the centroid) where the stress changes from compression to tension (Fig. A2.6). It may also vary between cross-sections due to variation in the bending moment along the element.

The magnitude of bending stress at any point in an element depends on four factors, namely the bending moment at the cross-

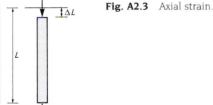

Fig. A2.3   Axial strain.

Axial strain = $\frac{\Delta L}{L}$

Fig. A2.4   Shear strain.

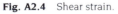

(a)

(b)

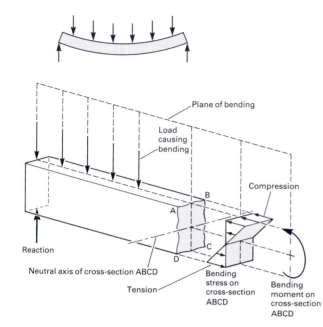

Plane of bending

Load
causing
bending

Compression

B

A

Reaction

Neutral axis of cross-section ABCD

Tension

Bending
stress on
cross-section
ABCD

Bending
moment on
cross-section
ABCD

C

D

Fig. A2.6 Distribution of bending stress on a cross-section of an element carrying a bending-type load. (a) Deflected shape. Compressive stress occurs on the inside of the curve (upper half of the cross-section) and tensile stress on the outside of the curve. (b) Cut-away diagram. Shear force and shear stress are not shown.

section in which the point is situated, the size of the cross-section, the shape of the cross-section and the location of the point within the cross-section. The relationship between these parameters is

$$f = My/I$$

where: f = bending stress at a distance y from the neutral axis of the cross-section (the axis through the centroid)

M = bending moment at the cross-section

I = the second moment of area of the cross-section about the axis through its centroid; this depends on both the size and the shape of the cross-section.

This relationship allows the bending stress at any level in any element cross-section to be calculated from the bending moment at that

cross-section. It is equivalent to the axial stress formula $f = P/A$.

The equation stated above is called the elastic bending formula. It is only valid in the elastic range (see Section A2.4). It is one of the most important relationships in the theory of structures and it is used in a variety of forms, in the design calculations of structural elements which are subjected to bending-type loads. A number of points may be noted in connection with this equation:

1 The property of a beam cross-section on which the relationship between bending moment and bending stress depends is its second moment of area (I) about the particular axis through its centroid which is normal to the plane in which the bending loads lie. This axis is the neutral axis of the beam.

   I is a property of the shape of the cross-section. Its definition is

$$I = \int y^2 dA$$

For those who are not mathematically minded Fig. A2.7 may make the meaning of the term more clear. The second moment of area of a cross-section about the axis through its centroid can be evaluated by breaking up the total area into small parts.

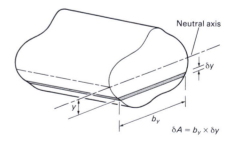

Neutral axis

δy

y

b_y

$\delta A = b_y \times \delta y$

Fig. A2.7 A short length of beam with a cross-section of indeterminate shape is shown here. The contribution which the shaded strip of cross-section makes to the resistance of bending is proportional to $\partial I = y^2 \partial A$. The ability of the whole cross-section to resist bending is the sum of the contributions of the elemental areas of the cross-section:

$I = \Sigma y^2 \partial A$

If ∂A is small this becomes:

$I = \int y^2 \partial A.$

The second moment of area of any part about the centroidal axis is simply the area of the part multiplied by the square of its distance from the axis. The second moment of area of the whole cross-section is the sum of all of the small second moments of area of the parts.

The reason why this rather strange quantity I, which is concerned with the distribution of the area of the cross-section with respect to its centroidal axis, determines the bending resistance of the beam is that the size of the contribution which each piece of material within the cross-section makes to the total bending resistance depends on its remoteness from the neutral axis (more precisely on the square of its distance from the neutral axis).

The bending strength of a cross-section therefore depends on the extent to which the material in it is dispersed away from the neutral axis and I is the measure of this. Fig. A2.8 shows three beam cross-sections, all of the same total area. (a) is stronger in bending with respect to the X–X axis than (b), which is stronger than (c), despite the fact that the total cross-sectional area of each is the same; this is because (a) has the largest I about the X–X axis, (b) the next largest and (c) the smallest.

The efficiency of a beam in resisting a bending-type load depends on the relationship between the second moment of area of its cross-section and its total area of cross-section. I determines the bending strength and A the weight (i.e. the total amount of material present).

2 The elastic bending formula is used to calculate the bending stress at any fibre a distance y from the neural axis of a beam cross-section. The maximum stresses occur at the extreme fibres, where the values of y are greatest, and, for the purpose of calculating extreme fibre stresses, the equation is frequently written in the form,

$$f_{max} = M/Z$$

where: $Z = I/y_{max}$

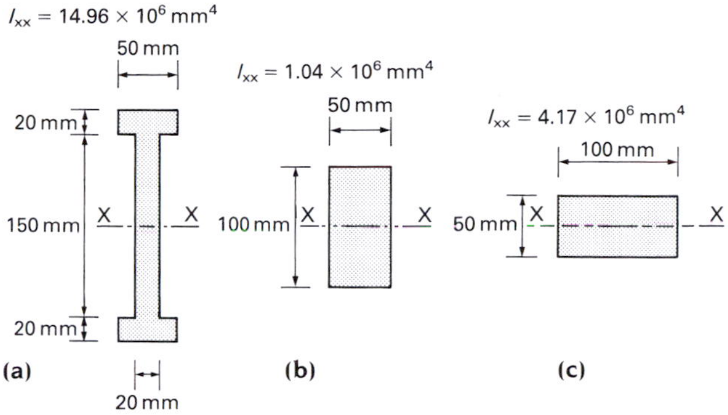

$I_{xx} = 14.96 \times 10^6 \text{ mm}^4$

$I_{xx} = 1.04 \times 10^6 \text{ mm}^4$

$I_{xx} = 4.17 \times 10^6 \text{ mm}^4$

Fig. A2.8 All of these beam cross-sections have the same area of 5000 mm² but (a) has the greatest bending strength about the X–X axis because it has the largest I_{x-x}.

Z is called the modulus of the cross-section. (It is often referred to as the 'section modulus'; sometimes the term 'elastic modulus' is used and this is unfortunate because it leads to confusion with the term 'modulus of elasticity' – see Section A2.4.)

If the cross-section of an element is not symmetrical about the axis through its centroid the maximum stresses in tension and compression are different. Where this occurs two section moduli are quoted for the cross-section, one for each value of y_{max}.)

3 In the form $M = fI/y$ or $M = fZ$ the elastic bending formula can be used, in conjunction with a relevant allowable stress value, to calculate the maximum value of bending moment which a beam cross-section can resist. This is called the 'moment of resistance' of the cross-section.

4 In the form

$$Z_{req} = M_{max}/f_{max}$$

where: Z_{req} = modulus of cross-section required for adequate strength

M_{max} = bending moment caused by maximum load

f_{max} = maximum allowable stress

the formula can be used to determine the size of cross-section required for a particular

137

beam. This is an essential stage in element-sizing calculations.

A2.4 Strain

To understand the causes of strain it is necessary to appreciate how structural material responds when load is applied to it. Its behaviour is in fact similar to that of a spring (Fig. A2.9).

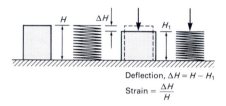

Deflection, $\Delta H = H - H_1$

Strain $= \dfrac{\Delta H}{H}$

Fig. A2.9 Deformation following the application of load. The behaviour of a block of material is similar to that of a spring.

In the unloaded state it is at rest; it has a particular length and occupies a particular volume. If a compressive load is applied, as in Fig. A2.9, there is at first nothing to resist it; the material in the immediate locality of the load simply deforms under its action and the ends of the element move closer together. This has the effect of generating internal force in the material which resists the load and attempts to return the element to its original length. The magnitude of the resisting force increases as the deformation increases and the movement ceases when sufficient deformation has occurred to generate enough internal force to resist totally the applied load. Equilibrium is then established with the element carrying the load, but only after it has suffered a certain amount of deformation.

The important point here is that the resistance of load can occur only if deformation of material also occurs; a structure can therefore be regarded as something which is animate and which moves either when a load is applied to it or if the load changes. The need to prevent the movement

from being excessive is a consideration which influences structural design.

The relationship between stress and strain is one of the fundamental properties of a material. Figure A2.10 shows graphs of axial stress plotted against axial strain for steel and concrete. In both cases the graph is a straight line in the initial stages of loading, the so-called 'elastic' range, and a curve in the higher loading range, which is called the 'inelastic' or 'plastic' range. In the elastic range the stress is directly proportional to the strain and the ratio of stress to strain, which is the gradient of the graph, is constant and is called the 'modulus of elasticity' of the material (E).

In the inelastic range the amount of deformation which occurs for a given increase in load is greater than in the elastic range. A further difference between the two ranges is that if the load is released after the inelastic range has been entered the specimen does not return to its original length: a permanent

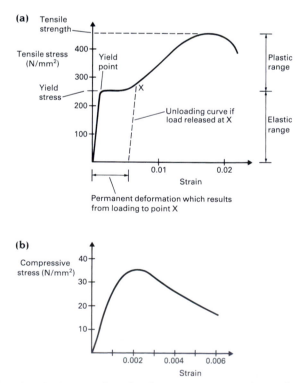

Fig. A2.10 Typical graphs of stress against strain for steel and concrete. (a) Steel. (b) Concrete.

deformation occurs and the material is said to have 'yielded'. In the case of steel the transition between elastic and inelastic behaviour occurs at a well-defined level of stress, called the yield stress. Concrete produces a more gradual transition. If a specimen of either material is subjected to a load which increases indefinitely a failure stress is eventually reached; the magnitude of this is usually significantly greater than the yield stress.

The modulus of elasticity is one of the fundamental properties of a material. If it is high, a small amount of deformation only is required to produce a given amount of stress and therefore to resist a given amount of load. Such materials feel hard to the touch; steel and stone are examples. Where the modulus of elasticity of a material is low the amount of deformation which occurs before a load is resisted is high; this gives the material, rubber for example, a soft feel.

A further point in connection with stress and strain is that the load/deflection graphs for complete structures are similar to the stress/strain graphs for the materials from which they are made. When the stress in the material in a complete structure is within the elastic range, the load/deflection graph for the structure as a whole is a straight line and the behaviour of the structure is said to be linear. If the material in the structure is stressed in the inelastic range the load/deflection relationship for the whole structure will not be a straight line and the structure is said to exhibit non-linear behaviour.

Appendix 3

The concept of statical determinacy

A3.1 Introduction

It has been shown that the conditions for equilibrium of a set of coplanar forces can be summarised in the three equations of equilibrium (see Appendix 1). These equations can be solved as a simultaneous set for the forces in a force system which are unknown as was shown in connection with Fig. A1.9.

A structure which can be fully solved from the equations of equilibrium in this way is said to be statically determinate. The structure in Fig. A3.1, which has four external reactions, cannot be solved by this method because the number of unknown reactions is greater than the number of equations which can be derived by considering the equilibrium of the external force system. The structure in Fig. A3.2 is also insoluble by equilibrium due to the fact that the number of internal forces which it contains is greater than the number of independent equations which can be derived by considering only the equilibrium of all possible 'free-body-diagrams'. These structures are said to be statically indeterminate.

Structures can therefore be subdivided into two categories, those which are statically determinate and those which are statically indeterminate. The two types behave in significantly different ways in response to load and the decision as to which should be adopted in a particular situation is an important aspect of structural design. Most structural geometries can be produced in either form and the designer of a structure must take a conscious decision as to which type is appropriate. The choice affects the detailed geometry of the structure and can influence the selection of the structural material.

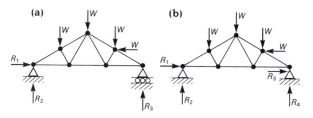

Fig. A3.1 The framework (a) is statically determinate. Framework (b) is statically indeterminate because the four external reactions cannot be solved from the three equations of equilibrium which can be derived.

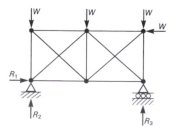

Fig. A3.2 Although the external force system of this structure is statically determinate the framework is statically indeterminate because it contains more elements than are required for internal stability. It will not be possible to solve the structure for all of the internal forces by considering static equilibrium only.

A3.2 The characteristics of statically determinate and statically indeterminate structures

A3.2.1 Internal forces
In Fig. A3.3 two independent statically determinate structures, ABC and ADC, are shown. They happen to share the same supports, A and C, but in every other respect they are independent. If horizontal loads of P and $2P$ are applied to joints B and D, respectively, the structures will resist these;

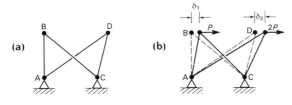

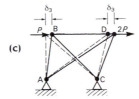

Fig. A3.3 The pattern of internal forces in a statically indeterminate structure depends on the properties of the elements as well as on the overall geometry of the arrangement. (a) ABC and ADC are independent statically determinate structures. (b) The two structures are free to deflect independently in response to load. (c) The presence of element BD renders the arrangement statically indeterminate. Joints B and D must undergo the same deflection; internal force, dependent on the relative magnitudes of S_1 and S_2, occurs in BD and this alters the whole pattern of internal forces. The final distribution of internal force depends on the elasticity of the elements as well as the overall geometry of the structure.

internal forces and reactions will be developed, all of which can be calculated from the equations of equilibrium, and the elements will undergo axial strain, the magnitudes of which will depend on the elasticity of the material and the sizes of the element cross-sections. Both joints B and D will suffer lateral deflections but these will not affect the internal forces in the elements, which will be solely dependent on the external loads and on the geometries of the arrangement (to a first approximation).

If a fifth element is added, which connects joints B and D, the system becomes statically indeterminate. The two joints are now constrained to deflect by the same amount under all load conditions and if the two loads are applied as before the extent of the resulting elongation or contraction of the elements will not be the same as occurred when the joints B and D were free to deflect independently. This means that the joint which previously deflected less will be pulled or pushed further than before and the reverse will occur to the other joint. A transfer of load will therefore occur along the element BD and this will alter the pattern of internal forces in the whole frame. The amount of load transfer, and therefore of change to the internal force system, will depend on the difference between the deflections which occurred to the two joints in the statically determinate forms. This is determined by the rigidity of the elements, so the distribution of internal forces in the

statically indeterminate structure is therefore dependent on the properties of the elements as well as on the overall geometry of the frame and the magnitudes of the external loads. The element properties must therefore be taken into account in the analysis of this structure. This is generally true of statically indeterminate structures and is one of the important differences between statically determinate and statically indeterminate structures.

The fact that element properties have to be considered in the analysis of statically indeterminate structures makes their analysis much more complicated than that of equivalent statically determinate structures; in particular, it requires that the rigidity of the elements be taken into account. As this can only be done once the element dimensions have been decided and a material selected, it means that the design calculations for statically indeterminate structures must be carried out on a trial and error basis. A set of element sizes must be selected initially to allow the analysis to be carried out. Once the internal forces have been calculated the suitability of the trial sizes can be assessed by calculating the stress which will occur in them. The element sizes must normally be altered to suit the particular internal forces which occur and this causes a change in the pattern of the internal forces. A further analysis is then required to calculate the new internal forces, followed by a further revision of the element dimensions. The sequence must be continued until satisfactory element sizes are obtained. Cycles of calculations of this type are routine in computer-aided design.

By comparison, the calculations for statically determinate structures are much more straightforward. The internal forces in the elements depend solely on the external loads and on the overall geometry of the structure. They can therefore be calculated before any decision on element dimensions or a structural material has been taken. Once the internal forces are known, a material can be chosen and appropriate element dimensions selected. These will not affect the pattern of the internal forces and so a single sequence of calculations is sufficient to complete the design.

A3.2.2 Efficiency in the use of material

The efficiency with which structural material is used is normally greater with statically indeterminate structures because the presence of a larger number of constraints allows a more direct transmission of loads to the foundations and a more even sharing of load by all of the elements. The benefits of statical indeterminacy in this respect are most easily seen in relation to structures with rigid joints, in which the resulting structural continuity causes smaller bending moments to occur than are present in equivalent statically determinate structures under the same load conditions. As before the differences between the two types of structure can be appreciated by studying very simple examples.

The simply supported beam (Fig. A3.4), whose supports offer no restraint against rotation of the beam ends, is a statically determinate structure. The deflected shape of this, in response to a uniformly distributed load, is a sagging curve in which, as in all structures which are subjected to bending, the intensity of the curvature at every cross-section is directly proportional to the magnitude of the bending moment at that cross-section. The curvature is greatest at mid-span and decreases to zero at the supports where the beam ends tilt but remain straight.

A beam whose ends are restrained against rotation is a statically indeterminate structure (Fig. A3.5). The fixed-end supports are each capable of producing three external reactions and the total of six reactions makes the solution of the external force system

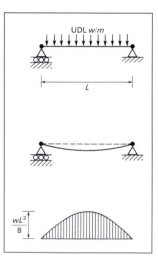

Fig. A3.4 Load, deflection and bending moment diagrams for a statically determinate simply supported beam.

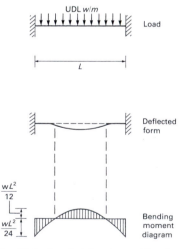

Fig. A3.5 Load, deflection and bending moment diagrams for a statically indeterminate beam subjected to the same load pattern as in Fig. A3.4. The effect of the restraint at the supports, which are the cause of the statical indeterminacy, is to reduce the value of the maximum bending moment.

impossible from the three equations of equilibrium which can be derived. Another consequence of the end fixities, and of the moment reactions which result from them, is that the ends of the beam remain horizontal when a load is applied. The mid-span portion still adopts a sagging curve, but the amount of sag is less than in the simply supported case, because a reversal in the direction of the curvature occurs at each end. The effect is seen in the bending moment diagram, in which regions of negative bending moment occur to correspond with the hogging curvature at the beam ends. The reduction in the sag at mid-span is associated with a smaller positive bending moment than occurs in the simply supported beam.

The total depth of the bending moment diagram is the same for both beams, but the effect of the end fixity is to reduce the maximum positive bending moment at mid-span from $wL/8$, for the simply supported beam, to $wL/24$ for the beam with fixed ends, where w is the total load carried and L is the span. The overall maximum bending moment in the fixed-ended beam is in fact a negative value of $-wL/12$, which occurs at its ends. The effect of fixing the ends of the beam and of making it statically indeterminate is therefore to reduce the maximum value of the bending moment from $wL/8$ at mid-span to $-wL/12$ at the supports.

As the bending stress in a beam is everywhere directly proportional to the bending moment, assuming that the cross-section is constant along its length, the highest stresses in the fixed-ended beam occur at the ends of the span and are less, by a factor of 2/3, than the highest stress in the equivalent simply supported beam, which occurs at mid-span. The fixed-ended beam is therefore able to carry a load which is 1.5 times greater than the load on an equivalent simply supported beam before it is stressed to the same extent; it is therefore 1.5 times as strong. Conversely, a fixed-ended beam which is 2/3 the size of an equivalent simply supported beam can carry the same load with equal safety. The adoption of the statically indeterminate form therefore

allows a more efficient use to be made of the structural material. As with most gains, there is a cost, which in this case arises from the difficulty of providing fixed-ended support conditions.

In more complicated structures, where many elements are present, the benefits of end fixity are achieved by making the joints between them rigid. Such structures are called continuous structures and they are normally statically indeterminate. In the beam which is continuous over a number of supports (Fig. A3.6), the continuity between adjacent spans produces a deflected form which is a single continuous curve. The hogging at the supports corresponds to areas of negative bending moment and reduces the magnitude of the

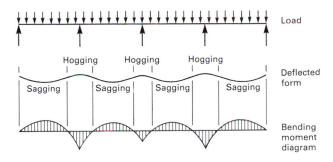

Fig. A3.6 A beam which is continuous over a number of supports is a statically indeterminate structure. The magnitudes of the bending moments in each span are lower than if hinge joints were provided at each support (the statically determinate form).

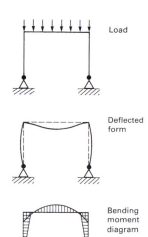

Fig. A3.7 A frame with rigid beam-to-column joints is statically indeterminate. The bending moment in the beam is less than it would be if hinge connections were provided, but at a cost of introducing bending moment into the columns.

positive bending moments in the mid-span positions. The effect of the hogging is therefore similar to that which is produced by the moment reactions which occur in the fixed-ended beam of Fig. A3.5. The same effect is seen in the rigid frame (Fig. A3.7) in which the rigid beam-to-column joints allow the columns to restrain the ends of the single beam which is present.

A3.2.3 The 'lack-of-fit' problem

With the possible exception of *in situ* reinforced concrete structures, most structures are prefabricated to some extent so that their construction on site is a process of assembly. As prefabricated components can never be produced with precisely the correct dimensions, the question of 'lack-of-fit' and of the tolerance which must be allowed for this is a necessary consideration in structural design. It can affect the decision on whether to use a statically determinate or indeterminate form, because the tolerance of statically determinate structures to 'lack-of-fit' is much greater than that of statically indeterminate structures. As in the case of other properties the reason for this can be seen from an examination of the behaviour of a small framework (Fig. A3.8).

The arrangement in Fig. A3.8(a) is statically determinate while that in Fig. A3.8(b) is an equivalent statically indeterminate form. It will be assumed that the frames are assembled from straight elements, that the structural

material is steel and that the hinge-type joints are made by bolting. The elements would be fabricated in a steel fabrication workshop and all bolt holes would be pre-drilled. However, it would be impossible to cut the elements to exactly the correct length, or to drill the bolt holes in exactly the correct positions; there would always be some small error no matter how much care was taken in the fabrication process.

The initial stages of the assembly would be the same for both forms and might consist of bolting the beams to the tops of the two columns. The resulting arrangements would still be mechanisms at this stage and any discrepancies which existed between the length of the next element to be inserted, that is the first diagonal element, and the length of the space into which it must fit, could be eliminated by swaying the assembly until the distance between the joints was exactly the same as the length of the element. The insertion of the first diagonal element would complete the assembly of the statically determinate form. To complete the statically indeterminate form the second diagonal must be added. If any discrepancy exists between the length of this and the distance between the joints to which it must be attached, the distance cannot now be adjusted easily by moving the partly assembled frame because it is now a structure and will resist any force which is applied to it in an attempt to alter its shape. A significant force would therefore have to be applied to distort the frame before the final element could be inserted. This would produce stress in the elements, which would tend to restore the frame to its original shape when the force was released after the insertion of the final element. The presence of the second diagonal element in the frame would prevent it from returning to its original shape,

Fig. A3.8 The 'lack-of-fit' problem. (a) Statically determinate frame. (b) Statically indeterminate form. (c) The arrangement is unstable until the first diagonal element is inserted. There is no lack-of-fit problem in assembling the statically determinate frame. (d) After the first diagonal is in place the arrangement has a stable geometry. There is therefore a potential lack-of-fit problem in inserting the last element in the statically indeterminate version of the frame.

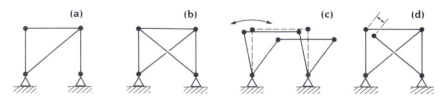

(a) (b) (c) (d)

however, and the result would be that all of the elements in the frame would finally carry a permanent stress as a result of the 'lack-of-fit'. This would be additional to any stress which they had to carry as a result of the application of the frame's legitimate load.

The performance in respect of 'lack-of-fit' is an important difference between statically determinate and statically indeterminate structures. Statically determinate structures can be assembled fairly easily despite the fact that it is impossible to fabricate structural components with absolute accuracy as any discrepancy which exists between the actual dimensions of components and their intended dimensions can normally be accommodated during the construction process. This does, of course, result in a final structural geometry which is slightly different from the shape which was planned, but the level of accuracy reached in the fabrication is normally such that any discrepancy is undetectable to the naked eye despite being significant from the point of view of the introduction of 'lack-of-fit' stresses.

In the case of statically indeterminate structures even small discrepancies in the dimensions can lead to difficulties in assembly and the problem becomes more acute as the degree of indeterminacy is increased. It has two aspects: firstly, there is the difficulty of actually constructing the structure if the elements do not fit perfectly; and secondly, there is the possibility that 'lack-of-fit' stresses may be developed, which will reduce its carrying capacity. The problem is dealt with by minimising the amount of 'lack-of-fit' which occurs and also by devising means of 'adjusting' the lengths of the elements during construction (for example by use of packing plates). Both of these require that high standards are achieved in the detailed design of the structures, in the manufacture of its components and also in the setting out of the structure on site. A consequence of the 'lack-of-fit' problem, therefore, is that both the design and the construction of statically indeterminate structures are more difficult and therefore more expensive than those of equivalent statically determinate structures.

A3.2.4 Thermal expansion and 'temperature' stresses

It was seen in Section A3.2.3 that in the case of statically indeterminate structures stresses can be introduced into the elements if they do not fit perfectly when the structure is assembled. Even if perfect fit were to be achieved initially, however, any subsequent alteration to the dimensions of elements due to thermal expansion or contraction would lead to the creation of stress. Such stress is known as 'temperature' stress. It does not occur in statically determinate structures, in which small changes in dimensions due to thermal expansion are accommodated by minor adjustments to the structure's shape without the introduction of stress.

Thermal expansion must be considered in the design of most statically indeterminate structures and the elements made strong enough to resist the resulting additional stress which will occur. This depends on the range of temperature to which the structure will be exposed and on the coefficient of thermal expansion of the material. It is a factor which obviously reduces the load carrying capacity and therefore efficiency of statically indeterminate structures.

A3.2.5 The effect of differential settlement of foundations

Just as a statically determinate structure can adjust its geometry in response to minor changes in the dimensions of elements

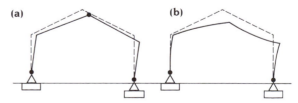

Fig. A3.9 The effect of differential settlement on determinate and indeterminate structures. (a) The statically determinate three-hinge frame can adjust its geometry to accommodate foundation movement without the introduction of bending in the elements. (b) Bending of elements and the introduction of stress is an inevitable consequence of foundation movement in the two-hinge frame which is statically indeterminate.

without the introduction of internal force and therefore stress, it can also accommodate differential settlement of its foundations (Fig. A3.9). Determinate structures can in fact tolerate fairly large foundation movements without distress to the structure. Statically indeterminate forms, on the other hand, cannot make this kind of adjustment without stress being introduced into the material, and it is therefore important that significant differential settlement of foundations be avoided in their case. The issue can affect the choice of structure type for a particular building. If, for example, a building is to be erected on a site where the ground conditions are problematic, such as might occur in an area liable to mining subsidence, the choice might be between a statically determinate structure on individual foundations which would be capable of accommodating movement or an indeterminate structure on deep piled or a raft foundation. The latter would probably be a considerably more expensive solution.

A3.2.6 The effect of the state of determinacy on the freedom of the designer to manipulate the form

Because statically indeterminate structures contain more constraints than are required for stability, more than one path will normally exist by which a load can be conducted through the structure to the foundations. In other words, the task of conducting a load through the structure from the point at which it is applied to the foundations is shared between the various structural elements. This does not occur with statically determinate structures in which there is normally only one route by which a load can pass through the structure.

A consequence of the redundancy which is present in statically indeterminate forms is that elements can be removed without compromising the viability of the structure (the remaining elements then carry higher internal forces). This property of statically indeterminate structures gives the designer much more freedom to manipulate the form at the design stage than is available with a

statically determinate structure. In the case of a statically indeterminate two-way spanning reinforced concrete slab, for example, the designer has the freedom to incorporate voids in the floor slabs, cantilever the floors beyond the perimeter columns, and generally to adopt irregularity in the form which would not be possible with a statically determinate steel frame. The fact that statically indeterminate structures are self-bracing is another factor which increases the freedom available to the designer of the structure.

A3.3 Design considerations in relation to statical determinacy

Most structural geometries can be produced in either a statically determinate or a statically indeterminate form depending on how the constituent elements are connected together. The question of which should be adopted in a particular case is one of the fundamental issues of the design process and the decision is influenced by the factors which have been considered above. The main advantage of statically indeterminate structures is that they allow a more efficient use of material than equivalent statically determinate forms. It is therefore possible to achieve longer spans and carry heavier loads than with statically determinate equivalents. The principal disadvantage of statically indeterminate structures are that they are more complex to design and more difficult to construct than statically determinate equivalents; these factors usually make them more expensive despite their greater efficiency. Other disadvantages are the possibilities of 'lack-of-fit' and 'temperature' stresses and the greater susceptibility of statically indeterminate structures to damage as a result of differential settlement of foundations. These various factors are weighed against each other by the designer of a structure who must decide which type is more suitable in an individual case.

The decision as to which material should be used for a structure is often related to the decision on determinacy. Reinforced concrete is ideal for statically indeterminate structures due to the ease with which continuity can be achieved without the disadvantage of the 'lack-of-fit' problem and also to its low coefficient of thermal expansion, which results in temperature stresses being low. Most reinforced concrete structures are therefore designed to be statically indeterminate.

The use of steel for statically indeterminate structures, on the other hand, can be problematical due to the 'lack-of-fit' problem and to the relatively high coefficient of thermal expansion of the material. Steel therefore tends to be used for statically determinate structures rather than for statically indeterminate structures unless the particular advantages of indeterminacy are specifically required in conjunction with the use of steel. Steel and timber are in fact particularly suitable for statically determinate structures due to the ease with which hinge-type joints can be produced in these materials.

Usually the circumstances of a particular building will dictate the choice of structure type and material. If a building is of small or moderately large size with no very large spans then the simplicity of the statically determinate form will normally favour its use. If very high structural efficiency is required to achieve long spans or simply to provide an elegant structural form then this might favour the use of statical indeterminacy in conjunction with a strong material such as steel. The resulting structure would be expensive, however. Where relatively high efficiency is required to carry very heavy loads then a statically indeterminate structure in reinforced concrete might be the best choice. If a structure is to be placed on a site on which differential settlement is likely to occur, the use of a statically determinate form in conjunction with a suitable material such as timber or steel would probably be appropriate. The decision on the type of structure is therefore taken in conjunction with the decision on structural material, and both are dependent on the individual circumstances of the building concerned.

Index